ROUTLEDGE LIBRARY EDITIONS: SCOTLAND

Volume 22

ENGLAND AND SCOTLAND

ENGLAND AND SCOTLAND
1560–1707

DOUGLAS NOBBS

LONDON AND NEW YORK

First published in 1952 by Hutchinson's University Library

This edition first published in 2022
by Routledge
2 Park Square, Milton Park, Abingdon, Oxon OX14 4RN

and by Routledge
605 Third Avenue, New York, NY 10158

Routledge is an imprint of the Taylor & Francis Group, an informa business

© 1952 Douglas Nobbs

All rights reserved. No part of this book may be reprinted or reproduced or utilised in any form or by any electronic, mechanical, or other means, now known or hereafter invented, including photocopying and recording, or in any information storage or retrieval system, without permission in writing from the publishers.

Trademark notice: Product or corporate names may be trademarks or registered trademarks, and are used only for identification and explanation without intent to infringe.

British Library Cataloguing in Publication Data
A catalogue record for this book is available from the British Library

ISBN: 978-1-03-206184-9 (Set)
ISBN: 978-1-00-321338-3 (Set) (ebk)
ISBN: 978-1-03-207372-9 (Volume 22) (hbk)
ISBN: 978-1-03-207376-7 (Volume 22) (pbk)
ISBN: 978-1-00-320659-0 (Volume 22) (ebk)

DOI: 10.4324/9781003206590

Publisher's Note
The publisher has gone to great lengths to ensure the quality of this reprint but points out that some imperfections in the original copies may be apparent.

Disclaimer
The publisher has made every effort to trace copyright holders and would welcome correspondence from those they have been unable to trace.

ENGLAND AND SCOTLAND
1560-1707

by
DOUGLAS NOBBS
M.A.
LECTURER IN POLITICAL SCIENCE,
UNIVERSITY OF EDINBURGH

HUTCHINSON'S UNIVERSITY LIBRARY
Hutchinson House, London, W.1.
New York   Melbourne   Sydney   Cape Town

First Published - 1952

*Printed in Great Britain by
William Brendon and Son, Ltd.
The Mayflower Press (late of Plymouth)
at Bushey Mill Lane
Watford, Herts.*

CONTENTS

	Introduction	*Page*	vii
Chapter I	A "Mute" Commonwealth		23
II	The Tudor Commonwealth		48
III	The Conservative Revolution		77
IV	The Radical Revolution		98
V	The Bloodless Revolution		129
VI	The Union of 1707		157
	Reading List		169
	Index		171

INTRODUCTION

FROM the time of Elizabeth's accession to the English throne, the problem of her successor was almost as important in Scotland as in England. It had played a great part in the politics of Mary Stewart's reign, and was even more decisive in its influence upon the policy of James VI. He governed his own Kingdom with an eye to his succession in England. To further his chances, he was careful not to compromise his claim by too definite a policy of his own, even though he tended to alienate his more extreme protestant subjects. He sought to conciliate; he relied upon balancing the forces in the two countries. He avoided imposing any strain which might lead England to set aside the only real claim which he had—that of blood. Dissension or dispute, unpopularity or national hostility, would have called his claim into question and given rise to a parliamentary decision as in the case of Elizabeth, or what was even more possible, to Elizabeth herself nominating another to succeed her.

It was in part because James had striven so hard for peaceful and harmonious relations between Scotland and England that his succession was accepted by both countries. As king in Scotland, he had already sought to model his own government more closely upon that of England, especially in the relation of church and state and in the promotion of economic prosperity. He urged his son in the Basilikon Doron of 1598 to "attract your kingdoms to follow the fashions of that realm of yours that yee find most civil, easiest to be ruled and most obedient to the laws". With time and leisure, and by the mingling of the inhabitants, such a fusion could be achieved.

It was with such hopes of union that James ascended the throne of England. At the opening of his first Parliament in England, he expounded his argument that because the two crowns were united in one head, so the two countries should be united in a "great Body". As it was God's will, that he should rule both kingdoms, "what God hath conjoined then, let no man separate. I am the Husband, and all the whole Isle is my lawfull Wife". He saw the unifying first of England, and then of England and Wales, extending by God's will to a union with Scotland, whereby the "one Island, compassed with one Sea, and of it selfe by nature so indivisible", and the two peoples united "both in Language, Religion and similitude of maners" should become invincible through their solidarity. The division had been "in apprehension, then in effect", and that apprehension was allayed by his rule in both kingdoms.

These were high hopes; indeed, visionary. He had much to learn about his new kingdom, and its determination to pursue its old ways. Two years later he had to address the English parliament again. "I desire a perfect Union of Lawes and persons", which for Scotland would be "such an Union, as if you had got it by Conquest, but such a Conquest as may be cemented by love, the onely sure bond of subjection or friendship". To him *unus rex* required *unus Grex & una Lex*. One king could not rule two contiguous countries of unequal powers. To England must the greater gain come: for Scotland subject to English laws must "become but as Cumberland and Northumberland, and those other remote and Northane Shires".

Whatever his hopes of union between the two countries and however keenly he felt the consequences of a bare union of crowns, James showed great caution in assuming the prerogatives and functions of the English monarchy. He expressly disavowed in the Basilikon Doron any experiences of English government, and later told his English parliament that it did not become him to tell it of anything "belonging to Law or State heere" until he had experience of "the particular mysteries of this State". He claimed on another occasion to have resolved to serve his apprenticeship of seven years in study of English laws before teaching them to others. But he never forgot that as King of Scotland he had given conclusive proof of his capacity to rule, and Scotland "doeth nearest of all others agree with the lawes and customs" of England. He was, moreover, "the eldest parliament man in Scotland", "an old king, not to be taught my office". Although willing to learn the "mysteries" of English government, his experience as King of Scotland had taught him the primary principles of kingship.

England welcomed James because his accession forestalled internal division and foreign interference, but Scotsmen were less welcome and union with Scotland was baulked by the conservatism of the English parliament. Some evidence of the Scottish attitude to the union of crowns is provided by Sir Thomas Craig's Treatise on the Union of the British Realms. He recognized that there were many in Scotland to whom the union stood for serious material losses and who thought that the king should have been kept in the country. Many towns were threatened by decline: trade was diverted; craftsmen as well as nobles sought the patronage of the English court. Union demanded the sacrifice of these interests. It meant also the rupture of the French Alliance, unseemly as that was and contrary to Scottish welfare. It involved English predominance, for "after all, the union will not differ greatly from a conquest in its results. ... Voluntarily and in the friendliest spirit we yield terms such as the bloodiest war and most conclusive victory alone could get". To London would drain the wealth of Scotland; from London would issue instructions as to government.

Craig did more than insist that these sacrifices were to be made. For him there was no question as to James' right to the English throne and therefore no question as to the duty of his Scots subjects. Every true Scot would have flown to arms to assert the right and title of his king: England would have been forced by war to take its King from Scotland. Craig counted it as Scotland's great gain from the union, and one which entitled England to exert a predominant influence.

Very few in Scotland, he held, had a real grievance. By the king's "wise authority" never was there less disorder in the realm. His privy council by which that wise authority continued to be exercised was accessible to suitors and just in its decisions. Nor was the king to desert Scotland: he was to spend there one year in three. The parliaments of each kingdom were to retain their distinctive status and authority, and their consent was necessary for the imposition of new taxation and the promulgation of new laws.

The subordination of Scotland did not entail the disappearance of its independence. Union ensured "a very firm-laid state", whereby Britain "has put behind her her misfortunes and calamities and lies harboured in prosperity and security". It could only prosper if it was controlled by a single, powerful monarchy; no state could survive where two rulers of similar power and equal following disputed its government. Union, therefore, meant the fusion of two sovereign states into a single realm, and, consequently, the punishment of dissension thereafter as sedition or civil war. No true union could permit disintegration into its former elements, and no true union could arise except on a basis of equality and freedom shared in common by all its members. The union of England and Scotland could only last so long as the agreement ensured the dignity of both and diminished the status of neither.

It may, then, be said that contemporaries were aware that the union of the two crowns in the person of James VI of Scotland resolved one set of problems in the relations of the two countries, but only to give rise to issues almost as important and assuredly as fateful in their history. From 1560 the two countries, politically independent, were mutually affected by the great forces released by the Renaissance and Reformation. They had become, in fact, interdependent. Political necessity and the adoption of the same side in the struggle against the Counter-Reformation compelled each to move in step with the other, but there was a great inequality in their resources and standards, and a marked difference in their social and political structures.

After 1603 there was little likelihood of political conflict between the two kingdoms unless, as Craig remarked, the Stewart line failed or the unequal treatment of the two peoples bred distrust of the union itself. But political association in the restricted form it took of the union of the two crowns was inadequate to settle justly the affairs of two peoples developing in different directions and at a different pace. Near-related ideas diverged in differing historical contexts, and the dominant ideals tended to become antagonistic.

These tendencies were strengthened by the accession of James VI to the English crown; by the policy of a foreign king in England and of an absentee king in Scotland, who in time became something of a foreign king there, also. He ruled England in the light of his Scottish experience and created and consolidated an opposition rooted in its English past. He ruled Scotland "with my pen, I write and it is done, and by a Clearke of the Councell I governe Scotland now, which others could not do by the sword". But in his relief at being able to leave Scottish problems to deputies acting in accordance with his instructions, he forgot that his own sensitivity to Scottish opinion, his greatest asset as King of Scotland, was inevitably dulled. Government "by a clearke" was apt to be understood as government by England. Confident of being master of his "craft", convinced that he was the teacher and not to be taught, he ruled in both countries as king of a party, and one which he largely created.

The history of England and Scotland between the union of crowns in 1603 and the union of kingdoms in 1707, was determined by the Scottish conditions in which James had learnt his kingcraft and by the English inheritance which he was never able to master.

* * * * *

In the course of the seventeenth century, Scotland developed politically and economically to such an extent that by 1700 a union with England closer than the union of the two crowns became possible, and, at least to some minds, a necessity. In the same period, however, the differences between the two countries were sharpened by the religious convictions which underlay the powerful presbyterian and Anglican traditions. These convictions affected much more than worship because the place of the church in society and the duty of the ruler to the church were in dispute, and the outcome involved the lives of subjects as well as of churchmen. Political and social principles of great importance were raised by religious claims. To be a presbyterian or covenanter, a puritan or dissenter, an Independent or a separatist, a High Church or latitudinarian Anglican, was to stand for a certain kind of society as much as for certain religious doctrines.

Scottish opinion oscillated violently between two extremes, between the ideas of an independent monarchy and limited church on the one hand, and a limited monarchy and an independent church on the other. Moderate men rarely attempted to outline a middle position, and certainly none were able to counter the literary and logical skill of the extremists.

The presbyterian tradition in Scotland began with John Knox whose attacks on the Roman Catholic church and appeals for reformation stressed the laws and liberties of Scotland as much as the true religion. In his *Appellation* (1558) from the sentence of the Scottish bishops against him, and in his *Letter to the Commonalty of Scotland*, Knox justified rebellion against idolatrous rulers and insisted on the duty of the nobles and lesser officers of the kingdom to lead the people's just resistance against all oppression. The authority of the ruler over his subjects had a Scriptural sanction and a Scriptural limitation; he was to rule according to God's law and in accordance with a covenant made with God and the people. Should the ruler fail to preserve the divinely ordered pattern of a righteous society, it was the duty of any, according to his station, to obey God rather than man, and to restrain, and ultimately to remove, all rulers, even the king, from office which was dishonoured by failure to carry out the divine commission. Knox's *History of the Reformation in Scotland* records his interviews with Queen Mary in which he boldly insisted that he taught no doctrine of disobedience to princes, but that of "just obedience, because that it agreeth with the will of God; and think not that wrong is done unto you when you are willed to be subject unto God: for it is He that subject people under princes and causes obedience to be given unto them."

Andrew Melville returned to Scotland in 1574, two years after Knox's death, and rapidly gained the leadership of the church, not only because of the skill with which he presented the case of the reformed church, but also because of the passionate sincerity with which he defended his principles against the worldly and selfish interests of aristocratic factions. In sermons, lectures and especially in his interviews with the young king, James VI, Melville sketched his ideal of a church and a ruler, each independent in its own sphere, but subordinate to the other in such matters as were proper to that other power. Thus, the king as a member of the church was subject to its discipline, and the members of the church in their civil activities were to obey the king.

Much, therefore, depended on the disposition of the king. The protestant nobles intended that the infant king should be brought up in the light of the true religion after his mother, Queen Mary, had fled to England. His education was entrusted to George Buchanan, a strong Calvinist and a distinguished classical scholar, who combined Scriptural and humanistic teaching in a theory distinguishing tyranny from true monarchy, and defending the right of the people to remove a tyrant. The *Rerum Scoticarum Historia* was written to prove that Scottish kings were limited by the laws and representatives of the people. In the *De Jure Regni apud Scotos*, Buchanan discussed the nature of monarchy in terms of general social principles, and his conclusions gained for him an outstanding reputation as an enemy of absolute monarchy.

According to Buchanan, the king holds office in order to regulate his kingdom by the principles of justice, and in a contract with the people promises to observe this official duty. The will of an ideal king should be the law, but since the will of ordinary kings is swayed by passion and partiality, it is only likely to be the instrument of justice when identified with the law, or what it is conceived an ideal king would will. The community by its representatives is to make general statutes for the common good and the king is to be their enforcer and not their interpreter. It is the inalienable privilege of the community to demand on just grounds the surrender of whatever power it has granted. If the king ceases to rule justly, breaks his contract, and shows himself to be an anti-social monster, that is, if he breaks the law, the people may act in defence of law, for the people is its author. As the enemy of the people, the king may be justly destroyed by collective or individual action.

Buchanan believed that the greater as well as the better part of the citizens would uphold the law against the king, but he was prepared to count as citizens only those who obeyed the law and observed the contract. The right-minded minority was the people, and entitled to act for it, even though the majority supported the tyrant. The extreme instance of the whole people accepting the tyrant as a true king did not affect Buchanan's argument which was concerned with what ought to be done. This last claim must mean that a private person was justified in killing a tyrant, although the people as a body was loyal, and must deny that the people was the author of the law. The people as well as the king was the instrument of law which was something superior to the mere will of either. The great problem which Buchanan's theory left unsolved was the human organ by which the true law was determined.

It was not until the Civil War had broken out that another book as radical as Buchanan's *De Jure Regni* was published by a Scotsman. In 1644 Samuel Rutherford's *Lex Rex*, the Law and the Prince, appeared and contemporaries fully recognized its influence. Rutherford was a leading Covenanter, and a fearless and fanatical minister. As one of the Scottish representatives at the Westminster Assembly from 1643, he had many opportunities of using his great gifts in the defence of presbyterianism, as he understood it, first against the Anglican church and secondly against the Independents and other sects. His life work was to wage a struggle on two fronts: against those who attributed ecclesiastical power to all church members and against those who confined it to a narrow hierarchy.

In long and able treatises he proved the divine right of presbytery, and rejected both episcopal and congregational pretensions. The same divine right led him to dispute the rising belief in toleration, and the equally dangerous doctrine that the civil power was concerned only with secular interests. Rutherford's ideal was the Scotland of the Covenant, in which the ruler was the reliable defender of the presbyterian church and the society directed by it.

The *Lex Rex* fits into this pattern. It is based on the power of the people, as reasonable and free creatures by nature, to choose the form of government and to appoint the rulers. No man is born a king or ruler, for every man is by nature a free man born. That some men are raised to political office, in preference to others, must be due to the consent and choice of their fellows, and this "natural liberty" is inalienable and indestructible. The people may not "capture" its natural freedom to choose because it may never abandon its right of self-preservation. Therefore, no grant of absolute power is ever valid.

Rutherford concludes that the choice of a ruler took the form of a contract between ruler and people, and that his power was fiduciary, by trust, pawn or loan. By this contract the people had a virtual power to compel the ruler to act in accordance with law, and the ruler had authority over the people. There was no need of a higher power to compel both to observe the terms of the contract, for, as in the case of contracts between two independent nations, each had the right to compel the other to preserve the contract. It was for the natural conscience of mankind to judge whether the ruler had subverted the law.

The contract is essential to Rutherford's argument. He is no champion of popular sovereignty, nor of the view that the ruler is the creature, the mere agent, of the people. The will of the people is not the active and unlimited force in government, and not the final or sole source of authority and of the obligation to obey it. If it was, democracy would be the naturally legitimate form of government, but Rutherford insists that the power to choose governors is not the power to govern. Government, that is, the order of authority and obedience, is of God; the form of government is determined by God in the aptitude of a community for monarchy, or aristocracy or democracy; and only the choice of particular men to fill political office is left to human will. The people's power is virtually, but not actually, government because of its power to choose those who command. A community is unable to punish itself: but by choosing rulers and by agreeing to laws, it consents to punishment through its rulers if it transgresses the laws.

The community has no arbitrary power; its law is the law of nature and not its own arbitrary lust. It is unable to grant a power to do evil, or to withdraw the just power of the ruler. There is no absolute power to do evil—only a power to maintain the law. The people's part is to replace rulers who abuse their office by such as know and observe the law. Even a king, limited as his power is, is not the people's deputy since in "the executive power of the law" he is really a sovereign above the people and, though owing his appointment to it, does not depend on it as ruler. The people has irrevocably surrendered the power of governing and cannot call the king to account for his acts of justice. Only as a tyrant is the king under the people's power. What is true of kings is also true of other forms of government. The people never surrenders its right of self-preservation, even to parliament.

Rutherford never explained how the people, incapable of governing itself, was yet able to exercise a "politic power" to meet and associate in one body to choose rulers, or, indeed, what he meant by the people. Later covenanting writings, like *Naphtali*, and *Jus Populi Vindicatum*, published after the Restoration, had to meet a situation in which the civil powers, including parliament, were hostile to the covenant, and, therefore, the appeal to the people was an appeal against parliament as well as against king. The people was then the party which truly understood and obeyed the fundamental law of reason and of God.

James VI was an acute critic of the defects of Scottish government, but a very shallow political thinker. He hated any form of contract and any possibility of resistance. In the *Basilikon Doron*, he justified the principles by which he had governed Scotland and advised his eldest son, Prince Henry, to follow his policy. In the *Trew Law of Free Monarchies*, James assembled a number of arguments, Scriptural, legal, historical and natural, which might give some plausibility to his contention that the king's power was unlimited and that his subjects must trust only to the king's respect for God's law. He did not attempt to give any serious explanation of how contemporary kings possessed a divine right, although he admitted that successful rebellions were possible.

The real defence of monarchy was undertaken by two eminent lawyers, men of great ability and wide culture. Sir Thomas Craig defended the right of James to succeed to the English throne in *Concerning the Right of Succession*, written in Latin, but published in an English translation in 1703, aimed originally against *A Conference About the Next Succession to the Crown of England* (1594), by Doleman, a pseudonym of the Jesuit, Parsons. Doleman's thesis was that kings were to promote the people's welfare, and that the people were capable of resisting a king who rules as he pleased. It followed that the people were justified in altering the laws of succession to a kingdom if the heir was unlikely to serve the common good. Craig was committed to James' cause but was not content to argue that James was more likely to rule justly than other claimants to the throne. Craig denied, as much on utilitarian as religious grounds, that the people were able to take any active share in government, and, therefore, to exercise a constituent power superior to the king.

Between Sir Thomas Craig and Sir George Mackenzie, who became King's Advocate in 1677, there was no great Scottish lawyer who examined the nature of the king's prerogative and the relation of king and parliament. Mackenzie had a sceptical and humanistic mind which was exceptional in Scotland before 1688. Interesting as are his literary works, his formal defence of absolute monarchy in the *Jus Regium* (1684) is little more than a clever exposure of the Covenanters' case. The principles on which he rested the claims of monarchy were taken from the common stock of royalist lawyers of the seventeenth century.

English political theory before the civil wars was limited by the success of Elizabeth's reign and by the uncertainty of the legal basis of the royal prerogative under the early Stewarts. Richard Hooker's *The Laws of Ecclesiastical Polity* (1594–7), aimed at the puritan movement in the Church of England, undertook to explain why the puritans ought to obey the properly constituted authority in the commonwealth, and in so doing revived the conception of the obligation of the law of reason as the basis of human authority. Government and law arose from natural sociability, but the form of government depended on agreement. No society was able to exist without authority to make laws. This power according to Hooker was delegated by the whole community to the properly constituted authority. The nature and needs of society justified such authority so long as divine and natural law were not transgressed.

The resort to arms against Charles I stimulated political speculation. Hunton's *A Treatise of Monarchie* (1643) interpreted the theory of mixed government from the parliamentary standpoint. The supreme power in England was the agreement between three co-ordinate partners, the king, the lords and the commons, in legislation; but he was forced to recognize, since there could be no final judge in the event of disagreement, that each subject must decide which side to support, if organized government collapsed. Henry Parker and Herle were prolific writers who in the years of the first civil war claimed sovereignty for the two houses of parliament, and were more extreme than the conventional supporters of parliament, such as Prynne, who wished to preserve the forms of the traditional constitution and to avoid any argument based on the representative character of parliament.

It was impossible to treat parliament as acting for the whole kingdom and not to raise the question of the people's sovereignty and of its relation to parliament. The agreement of the community to any authority exercised over it readily passed into the principle of individualistic consent. The claim of the people to an inalienable right of self-preservation, made by Rutherford, became the basis of other natural rights which the individual was bound to promote by social co-operation. The appeal to the natural conscience carried a personal responsibility for the preservation of divine and natural law. In the hands of the Levellers, Lilburne and Overton, the "people" became the actual body of men, subject to government by their own rational act, and equal to each other, at least in this sense that, being reasonable creatures, appeal must be made to their reason. The Levellers claimed that parliament must represent all adult males, act within a constitutional framework and safeguard the innate rights of the individual. A much smaller group of extremists, the Diggers, believed that reason demanded economic changes in order to achieve equality and freedom. The land was to be owned in common and its produce shared according to need. Winstanley developed this argument in his *Law of Freedom* (1652).

Republicanism found two great publicists in Harrington and Milton. Harrington's *Oceana* (1656) explained the decline of monarchy in terms of the transfer of landed property to the rising class of gentry. Parliament, he argued, was a popular assembly and its laws must reflect this fact. Arbitrary government in England was bound to fail. Government in a well-established commonwealth adjusted particular and common interests through the rule of law, and ended the power of some men to rule others by their own wills and for their own interest. The basis of the commonwealth was a wide distribution of land by which the public interest was protected against any usurping government. The government of the commonwealth was organized to prevent the growth of a strong and self-perpetuating governing interest. By rotation of offices, secret voting, and a separation of the organ for deliberating on policy from that authorized to accept or reject a proposal of the deliberative organ, Harrington expected the common good to prevail.

Milton's republicanism sprang from his passion for liberty as the means as well as the outcome of spiritual development. He defended the execution of Charles I in his *Tenure of Kings and Magistrates* (1649) and again in *Eikonoclastes* (1649), and *Defensio pro populo Anglicano* (1651). His argument repeated the familiar case against tyrants, and the lawfulness of popular action. He regretted Cromwell's clash with his republican rivals, and on the eve of the Restoration, in *The Ready and Easy Way to Establish a Free Commonwealth*, called for a council of the best men, elected for life by the people, to preserve the gains of the civil wars.

Milton's republican theory was not original, but his conviction that the best men would only appear, and their rule only be acceptable in a free society, joined him to many of the more radical sectaries. The plea in *Areopagitica* for liberty of thought, and for toleration and a secular ruler in *A Treatise of Civil Power in Ecclesiastical Causes*, and his emphasis on the voluntary church and the spiritual sovereignty of the conscience, were of greater consequence than the conventional argument against tyrants.

In the last decades of the seventeenth century, Sir George Savile, later Marquis of Halifax, discussed issues of policy and offered advice as to the proper line of political conduct in several pamphlets, reflecting his keen powers of observation and strong respect for English traditions. *The Character of a Trimmer* was an open defence of political expediency, that is, of a wise assessment of political forces, to ascertain what was least objectionable. The *Anatomy of an Equivalent* was a cool appeal to the dissenters' larger interests. The *New Model at Sea* defended a mixed monarchy as best suited, on practical grounds, to English conditions.

To Halifax, the issues which had divided seventeenth-century England were easily settled by common sense. It seemed obvious to him that the English king was greatest when king and kingdom were "one creature", when the governed were satisfied, and when authority was sustained by law and the voice of the nation. In practice, this required the co-operation of King and Parliament. The virtual consent of the people, given by its representatives, and the royal sanction given to the united sense of the people, ensured the active and willing co-operation of the governed with the government, because the people perceived in parliamentary action "their own will better explained by parliament". Laws so made were not to be resisted by private conviction but to be obeyed, until amended by the same authority as had enacted them. Halifax strongly held that "the advantage and sake of the majority" was the main consideration of all "public constitutions", and gave obligation to the laws. Legislators reflected the general opinion of what was advantageous, and were tied by nothing else. In every government there was an unlimited supreme power, with jurisdiction over everything else, but itself under no jurisdiction, and with power to make and alter laws. Behind government, however, was the people, who might have "nature on their side" and fly to the nearest remedy for any grievance.

Halifax was content that the majority's opinion of the general advantage should prevail provided that certain orderly constitutional proceedings were observed. Locke, too, argued in the second of the *Two Treatises of Government*, published in 1690, that consent, given by the majority, was the basis of government, and reduced the legislative power to a fiduciary one, regulating the executive on behalf of the people. Much of English constitutional machinery became acceptable to Locke when it was understood that the majority's opinion of the common good ultimately decided how institutions were to work. But Locke believed also in a fundamental law, in individual rights, and in a restriction of the function of government, all of which assumed that the majority limited its own will. In the *Letters on Toleration* (1689-92), he summed up the arguments of some of the bolder thinkers of the Commonwealth period, and gained widespread agreement for a theory largely denying the duty of the ruler towards the church.

The outlook of Halifax and Locke was more secular, liberal and tolerant than was as yet possible in Scotland. The disappearance of the religious issue from their political theory and the limitation of the government to civil matters permitted the opinions of reasonable men to be accepted as the judgment of the people in a way still foreign to presbyterian thought. Toleration and the neutrality of the ruler toward the church were ideas distasteful to Scottish minds. It was not until after 1688 that political theory in Scotland escaped from the influence of the Covenant and allowed a secular theory of popular control of government to develop. Until then, the "people" was the body of loyal presbyterians and its relation to the rulers was decided by the positive demands of divine law. In England, religious radicalism and humanistic traditions led to a theory in which the consent of the majority, assumed to be expressed in a constitutional way, and limited to secular matters, finally controlled the power, and restricted the range, of government. The secular state and constitutional government emerged together in England.

*   *   *   *   *

Political theory gives some indication of the issues between the Stewarts and some of their subjects in both kingdoms, but it fails to express adequately the less extreme, less logical and more conservative thought of moderate men, who rejected the extreme claims made for monarchy, church, parliament and people. It was just this body of moderate thought which was alienated by Stewart policies and acquiesced finally in the transference of the monarchy to William and Mary.

CHAPTER I

A "MUTE" COMMONWEALTH

It is clear that Sir Thomas Craig was defending the importance of Scotland at the same time that he defended the union with England. A lasting union meant an equal status, and Craig proudly championed the right of Scotland to be treated as the equal of England. Whatever the differences between the two countries, Scotland offered no less opportunity of a gracious and pleasant life than England, and in no other country were the necessities of life more readily obtainable. If its soil was less fertile and its grain below the English yield, the abundance of food supported a teeming population and fewer of its people died of starvation. When cereals were in short supply, highland cheese was available and farm workers preferred the superior strength-giving bread of peas and beans to white barley bread.

The export of the simple resources of the country supplied the country's need of goods which it could not grow or manufacture. The herring trade with France alone more than paid for necessary imports. So easy and profitable was the fishing trade, that it needed only the introduction of the English faculty of commercial organization ("wherein we confess ourselves their inferiors"), and its willingness to adventure capital in it, to establish a fishery more lucrative than any other in the world. A new attitude to trade and industry was evident among the younger sons of the landed classes, and there was only lacking the industries and skilled workers needed to teach profitable trades "to our poor men". In the near future, cloth manufactured in Scotland would be of as fine a quality as English cloth, and the industry was to be specially encouraged if the trade decline following the Union was to be stopped.

In terms of national plenty, which for Craig was a matter of food and clothing, Scotland was almost the equal of England. In other and less material directions, neither country was superior to the other. Although the English disclaimed Roman law and believed in the indigenous character of their own legal system, it shared with Scottish law the same fundamental principles of jurisprudence, derived from feudal law, and appealing to Roman law where any issue was obscure. In religious doctrine, likewise, despite superficial differences, there was "a solid foundation of uniformity". The differences in the forms of public worship were immaterial since "both churches have honestly endeavoured to get back to the form of the original institution" given in the Scriptures. The form of secular government was similar. Monarchy, independent and of equal status, ruled in each country. In resources and institutions, Craig admitted no real inequality between, and therefore no obstacle to the union of, the two kingdoms.

In this account of the economic resources of Scotland, the stress is upon the comparative simplicity of organization, the predominantly agricultural interests of the country, the reliance upon the raw materials and the small, though prospectively important trading and manufacturing community. The wealth of Scotland was in the abundance of its flocks and herds, and in their products which could be exported: in the wool and hides, in the leather and rough plaids. These exports, together with salted herring, paid for the wines and finely manufactured goods which were in increasing demand among the upper classes.

The growth in this demand for imported luxury goods characterized the last half of the sixteenth century. Scottish society learnt different standards of living from its contacts with foreign countries, and became aware of a greater refinement and increasing splendour to which it was in turn compelled to aspire. From the crown downwards, the resources of all ranks of society were insufficient to maintain social contacts with their equals in other countries. There was an extreme need of money which affected the policy of the king and the nobles, and therefore the lives of all those groups in society largely dependent on them.

Foreign travellers noted much the same points, although more critical in general of the relative backwardness of agricultural methods and the quality of manufactures. Communications were difficult and transport inadequate. Many parts of the country were very isolated, the Highlands especially being treated by the Lowlands as almost beyond social improvement. The sea had already been adopted by the Scots as the readiest, if not the least dangerous, method of communication with different parts of the mainland, and of exchange with foreign countries, mainly along the north-west coastline of Europe.

Wealth and power went with the land, and in the predominantly feudal society of Scotland the nobility as the greatest holders of land wielded the greatest influence. The Scottish nobility played a decisive part in all national crises of the sixteenth and seventeenth centuries, largely determining the balance of the other forces in the realm. Feudalism was prolonged in Scotland by the necessities of politics and the inadequacies of government. National defence and a line of monarchs of great antiquity but broken by frequent minorities had placed great responsibilities as well as opportunities in the hands of the leading nobles.

As James VI was still able to tell his English parliament in 1607, the Scots army was summoned by proclamation, and owing to the lack of royal treasure, was forced to come "to the warre like Snailes who carry their house about with them". The pressure of war was still met by that form of decentralization and local self-help which is associated with feudalism and the feudal levy. The nobles provided the forces and the leadership necessary for the preservation of the country's independence and for the maintenance of order against the lawless people beyond the lowlands. Their households and following were very large. By bonds of "manrent", they gained the service of many of the gentry and peasants on neighbouring estates in return for protection by which the nobles became the recognized judges of their followers. The younger branches of a noble house usually gave support to the head of the family, even when by no means dependent on him.

Around each noble arose a specific interest which it was incumbent on him to pursue, both by supporting his followers in their troubles and by imposing on them his policy and methods of satisfying his and their needs. The conflict of these interests accounts for much of the lawlessness of Scottish society in the last half of the sixteenth century. When a noble dared a sudden raid on the king in Holyrood House, when the king's person could be seized by a group of "patriotic" nobles, when feuds between noble houses led to serious disorders in the streets of Edinburgh, then it is not surprising that farther afield and between the nobles themselves petty warfare was common.

The power of the nobles had an official character. Many enjoyed a royal grant of barony, and some a grant of regality. By the first was conferred power of civil and military jurisdiction over an estate: to lead in war, and to be the judge. By the second, almost supreme powers over an estate were granted.

Such grants of power and jurisdiction were often necessary to ensure definite organization and administration in areas where the central government had little influence. In times of emergency, the nobles, strongly entrenched in their local connections, official powers, and estates, were called upon to vindicate the central government by using their local resources against the enemies of the crown. Special commissions conferring drastic powers were granted, and the rivalry of two groups of nobles might become a struggle between an officially authorized group against its enemy. The law was to be enforced by the resources of feudal power, and for that purpose such methods as were sanctioned by letters of fire and sword, were used with impunity. A lawless area was taught by savage reprisals the meaning of law.

The power of some noble houses, such as Argyle in the west or Huntly in the north-east, was so great as almost to escape all real regulation by the crown. When James VI, as late as 1594 decided to assert his authority over the Catholic Earl of Huntly, he had to call out the feudal army as well as accept the grants obtained by the presbyterian crusading ministers of the churches of Edinburgh. Almost as important as these great feudal powers were the hereditary rights of many noble houses to what were still important offices of state. The Earl of Argyle was the hereditary justiciar of Scotland and as such presided over the criminal court to which his own enemies might be brought.

Commerce and industry played but a small part in Scottish economy. The towns were centres of small scale exchange and opened up some opportunities of foreign trading, but they were of little importance compared to the great rural interests of the whole country. The agricultural interests of the towns were large: in wealth and population the towns were behind the country. The cargoes of ships trading with the Continent were made up of a great number of small consignments from a large number of small holdings. The Scots staple port in the Low Countries existed primarily for the protection of Scottish merchants, who received certain trading privileges in return for which the port possessed the monopoly of trade through the Low Countries with Scotland. In the last quarter of the sixteenth century the use of the staple was restricted to the merchant burgesses of the royal burghs whose activities and occupations were narrowly regulated.

The old alliance with France had promoted certain commercial privileges, upon which the Scots, even after the Reformation, set great store. Their ships also sailed for the Baltic from their east coast ports, and to them was brought the timber which the treeless Lowlands needed so much, but usually not in Scottish ships unsuited to such a bulky cargo. Indeed, many of the ships owned by Scots were built abroad.

Foreign trade was well called the "Wild Adventure": the risks were great not only by sea but in the dealings of comparatively unprotected merchants in foreign ports. The sea had become the way to wealth for the hardy and enterprising Scots, but their individual and piecemeal activities, undertaken without political patronage, did not coalesce into any national plan of dominion by sea. The economic policy of the government until the close of the sixteenth century aimed at securing an abundance of goods for the home market and not at the encouragement of a great export trade, even though the interests of the great landholders were affected. It was only in 1597 that import duties were introduced. An attempt was made by act of parliament to maintain the stock of bullion by making it a legal obligation for merchants to bring back part of their profits in bullion despite the prohibition of foreign governments.

Such government policies, significant of a more ambitious outlook, revealed the administrative weakness which thwarted any policy of national power by economic planning. Royal officials were unable to enforce the law: one Edinburgh merchant forcibly prevented the confiscation of bullion which he intended to export. Other merchants evaded the law and government officers by using every means of deception and by resorting to unfree towns where there existed no machinery for enforcing the government's regulations.

Prices and goods were not regulated on a national basis but by the burghs, which possessed an important economic monopoly. The royal burghs, or those with a royal charter, had gained a well-established organization before the Reformation. Each burgh exercised exclusive rights in respect of crafts, trading, and fairs and markets over a wide rural area of which it was the commercial centre. In the sixteenth century the burghs were able to prevent the rise of rural domestic, or cottage, industry and to obtain a monopoly of foreign trade in the main exported, and in all imported, goods. By 1602 whatever paid custom was regarded as belonging to the monopoly of the merchants of the royal burghs. These privileges were upheld by the crown, partly, because the monopoly of the burghs ensured the regulation of trade and facilitated the collection of customs, and, partly, because the burghs bore a special share of taxation. Beside the royal burghs, there were the lesser burghs of regality, and barony, each of which had the narrow privilege of regulating trade within its own limits.

There had long been a high degree of co-operation between the royal burghs and a close approximation in organization and methods, but in the last half of the sixteenth century the development of a common organ representing all royal burghs gave systematic expression to the earlier and looser forms of concerted action. The Convention of Royal Burghs met regularly from 1578. By an act of parliament of that year, commissioners from the royal and free burghs were authorized to meet four times a year in any burgh according to their wish and "for sic matters as concerns their estait". This act, however, but regulated what had developed without any charter or formal act of political initiation.

The meeting of burgh representatives for consultation about common interests in trade, burgh government, and protection of members' privileges was the result of the initiative of the burghs themselves, though endorsed and in some ways made compulsory by acts of parliament. The Convention exercised wide powers of legislation and jurisdiction. It largely regulated foreign trade, was active in promoting and protecting the interests of its members overseas, allocated to the burghs their share of taxation, and intervened actively and continuously to prevent disputes and preserve a common policy. The Conservator of the staple at Campveere in the Netherlands was its servant and he was held answerable to it although he was at the same time the king's ambassador. It was responsible for the elections in the burghs. It was active in protecting the "common goods", that is the property, mostly land, of the burghs, and to prevent its alienation. It was unsuccessful in its opposition to the new import duties of 1597 and failed in its earlier experiment of leasing the customs from the king in 1582.

The Convention of Royal Burghs was, therefore, the main instrument in regulating trade, in achieving a common direction of burghal policy, and in upholding the privileges of its members. It rapidly became the organ by which the policy of the trading community was formulated and given public expression. The burgess representatives in parliament acted as its representatives and their activity in parliament was determined at a meeting of the Convention held before a parliamentary session.

Although the Convention was the recognized and largely autonomous organization of the urban interest, even influencing parliament, always maintaining with much success the monopolies and privileges of merchant and craft guilds, neither it nor its members could impose a policy on the government and parliament when wider interests were affected. The import duties of 1597 have already been mentioned. Parliament also set aside a "pretendit act" of the Convention against the export of wool. James VI enforced his prerogative in relation to the burghs by frequent interference, as in his treatment of Edinburgh in 1582. When the town protested against the royal pressure to have certain councillors elected, the king named the provost as well, and gained his ends. After the great riot in 1596, the king's threat to remove his capital forced Edinburgh to accept terms which ensured greater influence to the king in its government.

In the closing years of the century a determined, though not a well-organized, enterprise was undertaken for the improvement of cloth-making. Its failure showed that Scotland was as yet unready for the development of handicraft industry on any large scale. There was no scope for a large industrial class. The balance of rural and urban interests had changed little in two hundred years. Scottish economy was much as it had been in the fourteenth century. It is this relatively static condition of its domestic life which is exceptional—it remained predominantly feudal in its interests and in the organization of its society. As yet the middle class was too small in numbers and importance to influence national life to any great degree.

These social elements and economic interests gave rise to the forces to which the parliament responded. It was essentially the passive instrument of the dominating group and until 1640 its passive role reflected the widespread apathy of the country towards parliament. The political struggle was fought out bitterly indeed, but not in parliament: it was a struggle of minority interests largely beyond any decisive control by the majority or by public opinion.

The people were too divided and too little organized to be able to exercise any continuous influence or to express any clear and final judgment. Not only was parliament acquiescent in its manipulation by outside pressure, but also the people had little interest in its proceedings and no urgent desire to reform it because there was little hope of it becoming the agency to voice, represent, and determine a national and popular policy, even by way of opposition.

This attitude to parliament arose in part from its composition and in part from its functions and organization. It was a feudal assembly of the tenants-in-chief of the crown, representing the landowners and the royal burghs, regarded as corporate tenants-in-chief. It was a non-popular and by no means representative body until the last decades of the sixteenth century. The nobles were summoned personally to attend. The freeholders under the rank of these Lords of Parliament had ceased to attend during the first half of the sixteenth century but in 1560, the critical year of the Reformation, the religious dispute revived the interest of the freeholders in parliament and their claim to attend was admitted on this occasion for political reasons under the deliberately indefinite formula that the estates included all "that are in use to be present". They were admitted to swell the majority, otherwise their claim would have been resisted.

As it was their numbers aroused fears of their power in parliament, even if these fears were somewhat allayed by their own desire to attend only on those occasions when their own interests were affected. The principles to which they appealed in justification of their attendance were of wider significance than merely legal and antiquarian argument. It was argued that the freeholders were the most numerous class and bore the greatest share of the national burden. No statute could bind any who were excluded from participating in its formulation. Other place than parliament in which the freeholders could serve the realm there was none.

It was only in 1587 that the desperate condition of the crown's finances led to a final settlement by which the freeholders of each shire were to elect representatives annually, whether parliament was summoned or not. Although the body of shire electors was small and exclusive, many neglected to vote. In the same way, full attendance of shire representatives at parliamentary sessions was rare.

These characteristics applied to the royal burghs also. The burghs were mainly controlled by a narrow and close commercial oligarchy anxious to retain its privileges. The representatives in parliament were elected usually by the burgh councils, and representatives in the sixteenth century had still to be trafficking merchants and indwellers. As yet there was little pressure by outsiders to represent the burghs; and the burghs themselves rarely sent individually or collectively their full representation to parliament. This may be the consequence of the powers of their own Convention, meeting independently of parliament, maintaining a separate interest and an exclusive attitude, and removing the compulsion to work with other groups to achieve a national policy. The burgh representatives played but a minor part in parliament.

Before the Reformation, the higher clergy had sat in parliament, and after 1560 the question of the clerical estate, with a right to parliamentary representation, became an issue of the greatest importance, both by raising matters of principle and by affecting the devious course of politics. Until the seventeenth century, the Scottish parliament approximated to the House of Lords rather than to the English parliament.

The organization and procedure of parliament was in the main responsible for electoral apathy. All the estates met in one chamber, but were so confined by the restricted seating, estate by estate, that little freedom of movement and therefore of parliamentary organization, was possible. Individual and oral voting led to a decision by the majority of the House. But parliament was not a deliberative and voting assembly until the experiments of 1640 demanded a debating chamber able to establish what was to be taken as law. It lacked, in the sixteenth century, organization, ability and experience. It was not called to play an active part in government but to select a committee of the estates whose task was to prepare the legislation which was sanctioned by the crown in the final meeting of parliament.

This mass of legislation, passed in one sitting when time would largely be spent in the reading of the Acts, permitted only formal approval, the ordinary members having very vague ideas as to its purport. The preparatory and all important committee was known as the Lords of the Articles and was representative of all estates. Initially, it was a means to convert a feudal assembly into an effective support for the government. It enabled elected representatives to take part in the king's secret counsels. Probably the widespread political apathy also accounts for the position of the Lords of the Articles, for little resentment before the seventeenth century was aroused by their activities.

Parliament was one of several agencies of the feudal monarchy. It did not possess the sole right to tax or even to legislate. These powers were shared with the Convention of Estates, which at times was only an informal meeting of parliament, but at other times little more than a meeting of the Privy Council, whether enlarged or not. It was distinguished from parliament in that it was not publicly summoned, and did not act as a supreme court of law, especially in matters of treason. It was careful not to exercise the peculiar powers of parliament. Its legislation required the usually formal ratification of parliament. It was able to interpret acts of parliament and to strengthen the executive by administrative action, which at that time permitted regulations of a legislative kind.

In general, it met on the crown's initiative to give advice, and the crown was until 1587 free to summon such counsellors as it saw fit. The initiative lay with the crown in the conduct of the business of the Convention of Estates which was limited by royal letters. A convention was usually more amenable than a parliament and less formal in its procedure; and its functions were sufficiently wide for executive purposes to enable the crown to substitute a convention for a parliament. That was just what James VI did: he preferred a convention to a parliament, an assembly to advise to a court governed by set procedure. It was even more than parliament a tool of the party in power.

The traditional pattern of Scottish politics was the struggle between groups of magnates for control of the means of government. These groups frequently constituted "bands" or solemn agreements binding upon all joining the group. Disloyalty to the "crown" or "realm" was frequently less serious than disloyalty to the band, for in times of monarchical weakness the "crown" and "realm" were annexed to a rival band. Possession of the monarch secured control over the legal processes of the government, secured the triumph of one band's policy, and compelled its rivals to plotting, if necessary, with the enemies of the country. Government by faction, the outcome of the excessive power of magnates, alternated with the efforts of strong kings to re-establish feudal superiority, but in either case parliament was little other than a court of registration.

This political pattern was only partially modified by the Reformation because feudalism was itself a factor in the Reformation, and consequently shaped its development, while being profoundly influenced by it. Parliaments and conventions were as much instruments of the successful party after 1560 as before it. Under Queen Mary, under the king's party after 1567, under the strong regents Moray and Morton, under "Captain James", parliament obediently set the seal of legality to any successfully asserted programme. From 1567 to 1584 faction prevailed. After 1584 James VI was aiming to master faction but was seldom assured of his success.

Moreover, the political sponsors of the Reformation, the Lords of the Congregation of 1560, constituted a band or illicit combination of subjects, and sought mastery of the political organization. The spoils of victory were greater than those accruing to earlier faction, for the secularization of church lands was the avowed policy of many of the protestant nobles, whom even John Knox could not restrain. The Lords of the Congregation co-operated with the catholic Earl of Huntly against the queen regent on terms which secured his position and veto over the settlement of church lands in his territory.

In 1570 it could be said that there were "none brought under the King's obedience but for reward either given or promised". Commendations of church benefices and lands were eagerly sought and were bitterly contested. In some cases, and in some parts, the Reformation was helped forward by the feudal authority of the nobles over their dependents. One historian goes so far as to stress that the Scottish Reformation was baronial in contrast to the English Reformation made by the crown. It was in part due to the strength of feudal authorities that the Reformation succeeded in default of a converted king.

However much the Reformation was dependent on feudalism and influenced by it, there was another aspect of it which led it necessarily to resist the full implications of feudal society. There could be no lasting alliance on the nobles' terms. The Reformation was the revolutionary force within a relatively static and feudally retarded society. It tended to become the cause of the middle class, the lairds and burgesses, and to awaken something more than preoccupations with monopolies and vested interests. It crossed feudal barriers and feudal ties, and drew the protestant nobles into a movement which feudalism could never hope to dominate.

A national interest, resulting in national division, raised rival principles and fateful choice. Religion, inextricably entangled with politics, was forced to challenge men's minds in more than matters of doctrine: the Reformed church was forced to seek to dominate the compromise with the world, if some compromise there had to be, and if none was to be admitted, then the greater necessity was there for the church to dominate society.

The Reformation was successful because of the weakness of the old order rather than the strength of its own supporters. Patriotism turned the Scots against the "auld alliance" with France when alliance threatened absorption. The crown's policy of support for the old church alienated the nobility, always fearful of the crown's reliance on the church, already suspicious that their interests were to be sacrificed in English wars to those of France and the church, and jealous of the wealth of the church. The failure of any royal lead to reform the church deepened popular indifference. The struggle was seen at first as a dispute between the nobility and queen regent, and the peasants gave little support to either. The population was in general papalist, and though anxious for reform was against revolution.

One section of the population, however, was affected by deeply religious convictions. The small middle class of the towns and the gentry in close proximity to it responded to the preachers, studied the new vernacular Bible, and prepared to assert new political claims in defence of their religious cause. To this class the Reformation brought a positive principle and a definite programme, narrower in conception and more rigidly held than the negative attitude of the anti-clerical, indifferent, aristocratic and patriotic elements lending support to the Reformation. The consistency of doctrine and the compactness of interests of this urban group gave it exceptional power in times of crisis, although it stood for only one element in the many-sided character of the Scottish Reformation.

In 1560 catholicism was overthrown and the Scottish Confession was enthusiastically accepted by parliament. Much more significant, however, was the rejection of the *First Book of Discipline*, the plan of the new church which Knox wished to see established in Scotland. The nobles had no wish to lose control of church property which by the *Book of Discipline* was to be restored to the Reformed church, but they were also out of sympathy with the Scriptural single-mindedness of Knox which left no room for "politic" reasoning, however pressing was the need to conciliate England or to make allowances for motives and interests less convinced than his own.

This divergence became greater still with the return of Mary, an "unpersuaded" queen and, indeed, as Maitland, the diplomatist of the Reformation, hinted, never to be persuaded by such methods as Knox knew. Until she had wrecked her cause by her impatient marriages, Knox thundered in vain against the nobles' concessions to her catholicism and to her scheming for the English throne. Neither nobility nor the mass of the people rallied to his lead. Only his own zealous following protested against the queen's mass and hearkened to his Old Testament vision of an offended God avenging Himself upon the whole people for their sinful compliance with the world.

It is this period, 1560–7, of Knox's dissent which is decisive in the history of the Reformed church and produced the conceptions of its powers which were to influence Scottish history till 1688. Denied political establishment, the church was given its basic organization as a voluntary society by Knox. Within the limits of its authority the *Book of Discipline* was put into operation. It escaped political control and was free to organize itself.

Although its membership was small, its loyalty was the greater, for Knox's conception of the church could appeal only to the minority. Its voluntary basis enabled its organization to be moulded by the whole-hearted co-operation of its members without being jeopardized by the claims of merely professing protestants to share in it. Its peculiar institutions were the General Assembly and the discipline exercised by the ministers in conjunction with lay elders. In this period of insecurity, when the Reformed church was fighting for survival more than for an ecclesiastical monopoly, these institutions served the invaluable purpose of guarding and expressing the individuality of the nascent church.

Knox stoutly upheld the rights of the Assembly to meet at its own discretion. "Take from us the freedom of Assemblies and take from us the Evangel," he declared: for in the Assemblies were determined the policies of the church establishing the terms of membership and the institutions of its self-government. For Knox the Assemblies established the meaning of the

Scriptural instructions for his age, and the discipline ensured a membership faithful thereto. The Assemblies were attended in a somewhat unorganized way by the laity of any importance supporting the Reformed church. With the commissioners from towns, provinces and kirks, the laity out-numbered the clergy. Laymen held important positions in the church itself, as superintendent, or bishop or moderator of the Assembly.

From the local kirk session to the General Assembly the laity played an important part, but it was especially in the Assembly that it found opportunity to develop its views, to take sides and make decisions, and to review all the works of authority in a critical and constructive way. The Assembly was the avenue to free expression of opinion by all ranks in the church. The secular privileges of the nobility were discounted in it; the crown's interference was hotly disputed; the middle class, unrepresented or over-ridden in secular councils, found in the Assembly the means to press upon the court and the parliament its own interests. Discipline reduced all to equal responsibility. Moreover, in the Assembly the laity were in touch with leadership superior to restricted lay interests and able to give an insight into the widest issues. Thus, the General Assembly was more aware of public opinion, more able to voice it and so more popular than parliament.

The claim to spiritual independence, including all jurisdiction and government, was forced on the church after its failure in 1560 to dominate the state. Yet Knox's ideal was not a church which was self-governing because it was a voluntary association. It was not enough for the believers to know God: the whole people was to yield obedience to God's order. It was not enough for believers freely to observe God's way: the obligation was divinely laid upon them to bring the whole community under God's will.

The Scriptures contained His will for His faithful. "The word of God is plain in the self . . . so that there can be no doubt but unto such as obstinately remain ignorant." Again, "if any object that punishment cannot be commanded to be executed without a Parliament, we answer that the eternal God in his Parliament has pronounced death to be the punishment for adultery and for blasphemy." God in His parliament had willed the law: it was contained in the Scriptures: princes and subjects were to obey God.

By such reasoning the sect of true believers was to strive to become a national church within which control was to be exercised by the true believers. For the national church, containing all inhabitants of the country, was to maintain the same standard, the same Law of God. It was for this purpose that the discipline existed and why it became the essence of the true freedom of the Reformed church.

Knox shared the Calvinist view of human nature. The discipline was essential. It had to be imposed. The co-operation of the political authority with the sect-church to realize on earth the order prescribed in the Scriptures was required by his ideal. It might be necessary to bring pressure on the ruler either through the nobles, or by appealing to public opinion of political weight through the pulpit. Fortunately for Scotland, the church had to use the public way of the pulpit and to seek the widest measure of support.

Calvinism needed a converted king and it never found him; nor did it ever find any alternative. The nobles, first in 1560 and then repeatedly, proved their incapacity for the role ascribed to them by Calvinist political theory. To rely on any party among the nobles was to incur the hostility of the rest. The mass of the people was indifferent, sometimes hostile. The middle class alone was loyal, but it was too small to be the source of political authority and the foundation of the state. Scottish Calvinism remained tied to monarchy, and although it was sometimes hinted that a particular monarch should be deposed, no reliable substitute was ever available. The dilemma of the church was cruel. It could not consistently press for limitations on political authority without making its ideal society impossible; but neither could it strengthen political authority without endangering its own freedom and authority throughout the land. Calvinist politics, like its political theory, was naïve.

The ideal of Knox significantly affected the representative character of the Reformed church. Its institutions had to be in the hands of trustworthy members of the church, not only excluding all who were of another faith as was natural, but also the merely professing Calvinist. While its institutions were to be representative, it was of the sect rather than of the nation. Hence, the body of the church was restricted to an expression of approval or disapproval of candidates put forward by the representative organs of the church. Upon this selective basis, the inferior organs elected representatives to the superior organs.

The Assembly was indirectly elected, and in such a way that the possibility of serious dissent was eliminated. In turn, the Assembly determined the policy of the whole church, transmitting its decisions to the lesser organs and holding minority movements in check. This system was called in the language of the times aristocratic-democratic. The polity was representative in the sense that the wider ranges of the laity were to be raised to the standards of the lay representatives in the church institutions who would then be indeed representatives of the laity.

Such an ideal and policy could not be popular as such. The church was too rigid in standards, too dogmatic in aim. It became popular by reason of extraneous causes. In times of confusion or in times of national discontent, the church stood for an independent and energetic policy. Within its institutions and under its leadership, opposition could be developed against misgovernment as by no other agency in Scotland. In this sense the church became truly representative, moderates willingly working with the extremists, but it had to be on the terms of the church. The more secular and more national opposition to governmental policy was forced into an ecclesiastical channel, tending thereby to lose its own character. It was only after 1660 when Knox's ideal was discredited that secular forces began to work independently of religious idealism.

In 1567, with the flight of Mary, the Reformed church obtained political recognition. The kings were to promise at their coronation to maintain the true worship and to eliminate its enemies. Teachers, lawyers, and political officials were to be of the Reformed religion. In organization the church was not episcopalian nor presbyterian: but its superintendents were not really like bishops although they exercised some powers of co-ordination over the churches in their districts. In 1573, Mary's party collapsed and the Reformation was finally secured.

The Earl of Morton, with English aid and the wholehearted support of the clergy, had led the king's party to triumph. But the unity of the king's party was broken by a disgraceful misappropriation of church lands by Morton and the nobles of his party. In 1572 the church had agreed to bishops in order to prevent episcopal temporalities being appropriated by the nobles, who, in spite of some jealousy of bishops as possible rivals, desired to retain their participation in parliament. This agreement was not observed: the bargains between the new bishops and their patrons damned episcopacy in the eyes of the churchmen, although the bishops had no more jurisdiction than the superintendents.

Morton as regent was a strong ruler. He forced the nobles to submission, imposed heavy taxation, and strictly enforced law and order. His imperious rule and his high estimation of the king's authority led him to treat the church as dependent on a superior political authority. He refused to treat it as equal to, or independent of, the civil government. He had one minister tortured with the "boot" and then hanged for claiming to speak with "the spreit of God" against Morton's government. In this he foreshadows James VI's policy but his fate was a warning to James to adopt different tactics: for Morton fell from office in 1578, and three years later was executed, because his aristocratic and clerical enemies combined against him.

The leadership of the church was undertaken by Andrew Melville, who returned from the Continent in 1574. By his efforts, episcopacy was condemned by the Assembly in 1580, as contrary to the Scriptures. He defended the freedom of the church from secular interference by developing the theory of the independence of the church in spiritual causes and of the corresponding independence of the state in secular affairs. In the *Second Book of Discipline* of 1578, the work of Melville, the church adopted this point of view, although in 1581 it had to abandon hope of agreement with the government. It was in 1581 that presbyteries were established to fill the place previously occupied by superintendents and bishops.

Melville withstood the will of Morton as well as, later, that of James VI, and in interviews with both staunchly upheld the church. Morton, after his fall, was accused of seeking favour with James by urging that he might be a "frie king and monarche having the rewell and power of all Esteates, quhilk the Kirk's General Assembly empeared", if he ruled the church by bishops responsible to him and repressed free preaching. Melville stood for a self-governing church in which its own assembly, without majority voting or a "led course", but by consulting God, by reasoning on the Scripture, determined all matters of ecclesiastical polity "all with a voice in an consent and unity of mind". But the clerical pensioners of the court dared not use their legal powers against the Assembly because of the "frequencie of barrones and breithring with so grait authoritie and zeall". Even as late as 1586 the Archbishop of St. Andrews was terrified by the number of gentlemen at the provincial assembly.

In 1582, James was accused of seeking the spiritual power as a new "popedom" and as if he could not be the full head and king of this Commonwealth without possessing both swords, civil and spiritual. The Raid of Ruthven followed; the king was seized by a faction of protestant nobles so that he might be counselled by the old nobility as were his predecessors and as the fundamental laws of Scotland demanded. But he escaped and was able to impose on the church the Black Acts of 1584 by which the king was declared the judge of all persons and all causes in the realm. No assembly was to meet without his permission and the pulpit was not to be used for political and seditious preaching. These measures permitted an attenuated episcopacy to be introduced once more in 1586, and a moderate section of the church began to look toward the king. But a genuine episcopacy was hardly possible after 1587, when by an act of parliament the temporalities of the bishop were vested in the crown.

By 1592 James was more favourable to the church, partly in consequence of fear of Spain, partly to pacify the country excited by his policy of avoiding a direct challenge to the Catholic interest. He abandoned his bishops, established presbyters in their place and confirmed the divine privileges of the office-bearers of the church, but the assembly was to meet only as the king determined. The policy of 1584 in respect of the king's supremacy was unchanged. Once more the church and king became estranged, largely because James' treatment of the catholic earls proved him to be no converted king. He insisted that papists might be honest folk and good friends to him. He resented the extreme policy of some of the ministers and at last, in 1596, summoned Black of St. Andrews, a courageously outspoken minister, before the Privy Council.

Black denied the competency of the Privy Council and the church took active steps to publish the issues throughout the country. The king tried to retreat and offered great concessions except for the formal principle of punishment, however light. The church held to its outright repudiation of the king's prosecution of Black, and James was forced to extreme and decisive action, much against his nature. Aided by a fierce riot and by the effusive loyalty of the Edinburgh craftsmen, he was able to take strong measures. The extremists were discredited in the church, and the moderates, supported by king and people, sought a less doctrinaire, if less pure, solution of the relations of church and state. A commission of the church was set up to act with the king for the good of both, with powers of jurisdiction in the church, instead of the disputable and external control by the Privy Council.

From 1598 to 1602, James tried to restore to the church its representation in parliament. Proposals that representatives should be chosen by presbyteries led parliament, in which the nobles feared a coalition of clergy and gentry, to support the king's plan of bishops appointed by him to control the clergy. Until 1602 the church sought to control any parliamentary representation but in that year the growth of the king's power was seen in the adoption of the king's plan. The Assembly put forward certain names from which the king might choose bishops in addition to the three he had nominated in 1600 without the Assembly's agreement. These bishops were, however, political: they represented the church in parliament, and had no place in church government. The presbyterian system was undisturbed.

Behind this confused struggle of king and the church, protracted over two decades, there was a conflict of principle which was to revive in the crises of the seventeenth century. In 1601 it appeared as a plea for the independence of the church. "Whar for sould our meittings depend on licences, letters and proclamations, namlie whill uther esteattes as of barrones and brouches, ar permitted to use ther privilege frelie. Sall the Kirk of Jesus Christ be les regardit, and restrainit in hir fredome and privilege, in a setlit and constitut esteat, under the protection of a rare Christian magistrat."

In the *Second Book of Discipline* of 1578, the independence of the church and the independence of the state were forcibly expressed. Neither was to interfere with the other in its own sphere. Neither church nor minister was to use civil means and powers. The state was politically supreme. It was a corrupt church that assumed civil powers. The church was the instrument of Christ's spiritual power—the only instrument—but it had no other power. Church and state were mutually exclusive and self-sufficient. Independence did not mean separation; indeed, they were interdependent, for each in its own peculiar way was to support the other. The civil power had to see that the church regulated itself by the Word of God, and the church was equally bound to see that the state provided justice and protected the church. Such co-operation was ensured by each observing strictly the divine constitution, scripturally recorded. The state was to command the church to observe the rules commanded by Scripture, and to use civil penalties. To the state belonged the sole right to use force on the bodies of men in order to regulate all external works for the sake of external peace. To the church was only a spiritual authority concerned with external actions because of conscience. It was to teach the civil power how to exercise its jurisdiction in accordance with the Word.

The Scriptural ideal was for the state to enforce the law of God upon the church so that it might be qualified to instruct the state how to use its peculiar monopoly of force. The state was divinely ordained to work with the church. But the state was not an abstraction: it was made up of christians under a christian ruler, and all christians were equally responsible for using their position to promote Christ's Kingdom, a responsibility exacted by ecclesiastical discipline. James was king but also a member of the church. None of his actions and policies escaped the disciplinary power of the church over his conscience. Melville clearly stated this. There were in his view no separate spheres of action. "Civil" and "ecclesiastical" were only different ways of dealing with the same matters. The king, as it was said in 1596, was to act "with advys of the watchmen, and at the sight of the Siers".

The ultimate issue was, as James saw, who was the judge of Scripture. "All your seditious deallings ar cloked, and hes bein with that name of the best men," he declared in one of his many interviews with the ministers. The ministers in 1596 argued that a minister might act "with the best part, which commonly is not the most" part of the kirk session: "for he being the messenger of God and interpreter of his Word, hes more authority with a few than a great multitude in the contrary". The "best men", the "best part", represent the extremism of the Covenanters, Protesters, Cargillites and Cameronians of the seventeenth century.

The practice of the Assembly from 1560 to 1596 was in accord with ecclesiastical theory. It intervened in executive matters, made protests against the king's ministers and laid down his policy. It acted against trade with Spain, limited usury and the exportation of wheat, and in other ways attempted to determine economic policy. Even the king's officers were summoned to answer before it. One of its delegates to the king gives the church's ideal succinctly. He tried to show the king that the church would do "anything for the King's pleasuring with warrant of God and guid conscience, and that by his throuche lyking and conjunction with the Kirk, maters, bathe in Kirk and policie, might go right and weill fordwart."

James aimed at being an arbitrator between the different factions and not the tool of any. He wished to follow a middle course, to be the sovereign of a whole people and to reduce conflicting interests to a national order under his direction. He enjoyed great popularity. He was given several public demonstrations of loyalty. But his resources were sadly inadequate. He had inherited a feudal monarchy which was administratively strong only when a strong king was on the throne, and a series of regents, broken by the reign of a queen, had gravely reduced royal authority. It is true that this personal and feudal power was on exceptional occasions very effective, but it is also true that such action involved prodigious efforts. When James overcame Huntly in 1594, it was by drastic and national measures; when he opposed the church in 1596, it required almost as drastic methods.

The institutions of this feudal monarchy were undeveloped, save for the exaggerated powers of the privy council. Conciliar government was characteristic of Scottish government. In addition to its wide executive powers, the privy council had legislative functions which were regarded as executive acts. It was not to make or alter laws, but acted on behalf of parliament in the intervals between its infrequent sessions. Its organization was relatively undifferentiated. Its effective powers were weak, especially in the remoter parts. The central government had as yet inadequate machinery to ensure administrative results in the localities. James VI himself insisted that the problem of Scottish government was to secure the execution of the existing body of good legislation.

The poverty of the crown was the most serious cause of executive weakness. Throughout the sixteenth century, the crown suffered from lack of money. Taxation was light. Feudal dues were inadequate. Church lands had to be disposed of, or granted to secure support from the nobles. Commercial policy restricted the king's power to increase revenue until the end of the century. James pinned his hopes of a larger revenue on industrial expansion and joined in many speculative enterprises.

James had by 1603 gone a long way to his ideal of "free monarchy" independent of faction, church and estates, enforcing law impartially, and directing all to the national interest. Strong monarchy was an essential of his times. But James' success depended on a politician's exploitation of conflicting interests, each partly needing the royal alliance, each partly repelled by fears of strong monarchy. Nobles, church, middle class and the masses were partially antagonistic to each other. No opposition to the king had a really national character. Were the balance to shift, were monarchy to become too strong and its policy too much out of touch with public opinion, then opposition might become effective.

Out of his experience and his vision of monarchy, James formulated his theory of divine right of kings—of a heaven-sent arbitrator, alone free to moderate sectional interests within a healthy commonwealth. The sole authority with a divine right, because divinely ordained, sprang from the pursuit of the common weal. It was absurd to believe that any section or combination of sections imposing their wills and interests, and displacing the common weal, could claim power by divine right: theirs was power by might only.

James was personally acquainted with government by faction and with monarchy grasped and exploited by faction. He knew that good intentions, embodied in legislation, were not enough, and that the commonwealth rested upon the executive being able to confine faction within the order of the common good. Therefore, the executive was the chief means and true representative of the commonwealth. To set limits on it was to weight faction and to represent a distorted interest. Only a "free" king was above faction, and able to determine the common good.

James might have identified himself with a faction—with the church and the middle class, or with a group of the nobility. His aim, however, was to govern Scotland by mutual accommodation. The free king, above faction, needed an independent basis. Although the strong kings of his dynasty had earlier shown the way to strain feudalism in favour of monarchy, and although royalist lawyers employed Roman law for the same end, the resources of the Scottish crown were inadequate. Unable to rest on might, James had to insist on right, first by emphasizing monarchy as the only means to realize the commonwealth and hence its divine right, and secondly by giving that right a secure foundation in hereditary monarchy, a right unaffected by the rightless might of factions, for then the arbitrator was heaven-sent.

In James' theory, the public authority was vested in the line of hereditary monarchs, all others in the state being private persons, whether singly or collectively, without any claim to exercise the public authority. They had given up by their own consent all their liberty. Who but God could judge of a dispute between public authority and private persons; otherwise a party to the dispute was also the judge. God had ordained the king as the judge, and made him answerable to Himself.

Moreover, the king was "the overlord over the whole lands", and so "Master over every person that inhabiteth the same", the "author and giver of strength" to the laws, which he observed only by his own good will and which he mitigated by his own judgment even if laws were made publicly in parliament, always bearing in mind that "the health of the commonwealth be his chiefe lawe". The laws were "but craved by his subjects and only made by him at their rogation, and with their advice". He made laws without parliament; parliament could make no law without him. Kings made the law, and not the law kings.

Private persons therefore, had the duty to obey, except where God's law was broken by the ruler, in which case they must fly without resistance from his fury and pray God for his amendment. For a "monstrously vicious" king would generally favour justice and maintain some order, save in particular cases. James was insisting that the commonwealth was impossible where private interests used the public authority: that the executive, the essential means whereby the commonwealth prevailed over private interests, was to be free to promote the commonwealth; and that active resistance always destroyed it.

Sir Thomas Craig held more moderate views than his master. He accepted hereditary monarchy and its absolute right to govern, but denied that laws could be made or taxes raised by its sole authority. The value of these restrictions on royal power was lessened by his admission that kings were responsible to God alone, that the subjects had no remedy and that the commonwealth without the king was but a "mute body", unable to take action against him. But Craig understood that religious innovations caused "great stir and resentment in the population", a consideration treated too lightly by the Stewart kings in the seventeenth century.

CHAPTER II

THE TUDOR COMMONWEALTH

THE tensions within Queen Elizabeth's England—signs of a rapidly growing society—expressed the conflicting claims and forces which were to end in the logical extremes of the seventeenth century. It was not until a hundred years after the final triumph of Elizabethan England over the Spanish Armada in 1588 that English society regained an equilibrium and was ready to take its place as a European power. From 1588 to 1688 domestic issues and the interplay of social forces dominated English history. Elizabeth's reign was to see the first differentiation of interests, the beginning of fundamental divisions, and anticipations of alternative solutions.

Behind Tudor greatness had been the mutually indispensable alliance of crown and gentry and towns. These middle classes had emerged before the close of the middle ages, had acquired some measure of prosperity and awareness of their needs, especially of peace and security, but had also learnt by bitter experience their political weakness. Economically and socially progressive, they were the victims of political exploitation. The Tudor monarchy provided the institutional structure and executive direction within which the defenceless but progressive movements represented by the middle classes were able to expand. Political obedience was the condition of prosperity. Collective action by a monarchy representative of the middle classes was the condition of pursuing their private concerns. Theirs was a passive role in public: they could only govern by proxy, by a strong monarchy.

That monarchy, in turn, drew its strength from their support and resources. The vindication of law and order and the application of policy on a national scale, often by arbitrary methods, depended on the king's appreciation of the only partially articulated needs of the influential classes. The political machinery of the central government was effective only through the ancient local institutions, largely in the hands of the gentry, and organized under the common law. All important as was the crown in the supreme direction of policy, it was limited by the conditions of local government, and by financial and military dependence upon the rising middle class. Strong monarchy supplemented and did not supplant the traditional system of government. Henry VIII's use of parliament revealed his connection with, and reliance upon, both the older institutions and the newer classes. Through parliament, their local significance became of national service to the crown. Tudor policy was to mobilize local interests and merge them in a national order: only under their strong government did the locally predominant classes learn and assume their national responsibilities. National co-operation was the result of co-ordination by the crown, and in that process the middle classes discovered their political strength.

In this partnership of crown and middle classes, of monarchical discipline and of social interests responding to new economic movements, there was a tension between the active direction from above and the spontaneous social forces from below, a tension which became acute in the reign of Elizabeth. The queen resolutely upheld the Tudor ideal of monarchy, claiming both the initiative and the ultimate responsibility for established government. Policy was hers to decide; her judgment was final. "I am your anointed Queen," she told her second parliament, "I will never be by violence constrained to do anything" since "it was monstrous that the feet should direct the head". She commanded her third parliament "that they should do well to meddle with no matters of state but such as should be propounded unto them".

As late as 1593, parliament was informed "for liberty of speech her majesty commandeth me to tell you that to say yea and no to bills, God forbid that any man should be restrained and afraid to answer according to his best liking, with some short declaration of his reason therein, and therein to have a free voice, which is the very true liberty of this house; not as some suppose to speak there of all causes as he listeth and to frame a form of religion or a state of government as to their idle brains seem meetest. She says that no king fit for his state will suffer such absurdities...." These were no idle words. She was determined to maintain supreme direction by the crown, to uphold its full authority and to leave judgment to God and the future.

Least of all would she agree to subjects prescribing her course of action. It was for her, mindful of her duty to God, to govern for the good of her subjects. "My heart was never set on worldly goods, but only for my subjects' good.... Yea mine own properties I count yours to be expended for your good." Her attitude was no denial of the earlier Tudor alliance of crown and middle class, expressed in the activity of king in parliament. What she withstood was parliamentary pressure upon her own office. The crown was to be the managing director, parliament to represent the passive shareholders. They were allowed to agree or to refuse proposals but were forbidden to promote counter-proposals of their own.

It was this negative role which was becoming unpalatable to Elizabethan parliaments, and to the energetic classes represented therein. There was no longer the same certainty that the royal policy was best for the queen's subjects and no longer the same helplessness to frame an alternative. Elizabeth stood for an older order which was proving too restrictive to her allies. It was this complication of the earlier and simpler pattern that caused the problems of Elizabethan England, for the factors establishing its greatness were the same that threatened its stability. The drama of the reign sprang from the tensions in the Tudor partnership, and the means by which the queen sought to control a society driven by its own inner forces.

There was much to be said for the queen's attitude. The condition of the kingdom to which she succeeded in 1558 required firm and energetic leadership to restore its unity and its power. At home, her difficulties were serious enough apart from the question of her own title to the throne. The coinage was depreciated, the treasury empty, and there was a lack of arms to defend the land. Her sister's unpopularity had left the people discontented and resentful. Religious differences were likely to lead to interference by the catholic kingdoms of

France and Spain, especially in support of the Stewart succession to the English throne. Scotland was still catholic and allied to France. England was in no position to resist a catholic crusade had it been launched under the auspices of the papacy. Quite apart from religious reasons, it was tempting to France or Spain to gain by one way or another, control over England and the balance in European politics.

It was by Elizabeth's genius that the danger of invasion was averted for three decades by which time the unity and power of the country had been achieved. She was greatly helped by the indecision and jealousies of her enemies, and later by their own religious revolts, but a false move on her part, a threat or alliance or hostile act, would have precipitated a conflict. A combination of France and Spain might easily have resulted from too definite a policy on Elizabeth's part. The complaint voiced in a later crisis that "if we prosper, it must be as our custom is, by miracle", gives one estimate of her diplomacy, a series of apparently meaningless moves. But the miracle was the way in which the queen prevented her rash subjects and her dogmatic councillors from taking decisive action, especially in support of protestantism abroad. Her policy was negative: to avoid as far as possible any commitment, any revelation of her likely policy, until circumstances compelled.

Throughout her reign, foreign policy was in her hands, not even her great secretary, Burleigh, being able to do more than to provide information for her use from his many continental sources, and to make the most earnest recommendations. So closely was foreign policy related to domestic issues, and so much were religion and politics intertwined, that it was equally necessary for the queen to deal firmly with those of her subjects who pressed her to marry or to declare her successor. Her marriage would have the greatest consequences abroad, and since her husband was most likely to be catholic, religious concessions to him might well have become the means to encourage catholic intrigues. Apart from the religious question, her marriage must have heightened faction. To have determined the succession might have produced civil war, or have endangered her own security. But it was in relation to the church and to finance, both vital to her foreign policy, that the queen's independent attitude and exclusive responsibility for policy were most evident.

Her policy in regard to religion was clearly expressed in a speech to parliament in 1588. Neither catholic nor puritan was to challenge her rule. "I mean to guide them both by God's holy true rule. In both parts be perils, and of the latter I must pronounce them dangerous to a kingly rule, to have every man according to his own censure to make a doom of the validity and priority of his prince's government with a common veil and cover of God's word, whose followers must be judged but by private men's exposition." It was the political issue in both cases which aroused the queen's unyielding hostility.

The papal bull of 1570, by which the heretical queen was deposed and her catholic subjects freed from their allegiance, ended the period of tacit compromise, and forced government and catholics to stand by principle in an interminable though spasmodic conflict. What was a political issue to the queen was a fundamental religious truth to the catholic. English catholicism was linked to the "enterprise of England", the schemes of the papacy, often delayed and obstructed, to overthrow Elizabeth. In consequence, the government had to fight for survival and catholic activities were treated as treason.

In 1572, puritanism, working in and through the established church, and gaining support as a patriotic movement against Spain and catholicism, began its campaign in the country and in parliament to change the government of the church. The puritans wanted the queen to re-order the church according to "God's holy true rule". It was the queen who broke the puritan movement, and drove it underground in the last years of her reign. The government of the church was a matter of royal prerogative. The religious ideals of puritanism were for Elizabeth a danger to monarchy and to the state. Therefore, she upheld her bishops, though privately in order to save her popularity, in their work of restoring the established church, and prevented lay opinion from endangering episcopacy and its power over clergy and laity.

It is noteworthy that these religious issues, and their political corollaries, only began to be critical in the second decade of Elizabeth's reign. For more than ten years the extremists had largely held their hands, waiting upon events and hoping that royal equivocation would yield to a more definite policy favourable to them. But the religious compromise at the beginning of her reign, cautiously achieved, and only taking positive shape in piecemeal measures, half-heartedly put into operation, expressed Elizabeth's policy. Once again her aim was to avoid positive commitments as far as possible and to obscure the differences between rival parties.

In the Acts of Supremacy and Uniformity, the ecclesiastical authority of Henry VIII and the prayer book of Edward VI were "restored", with such modifications as might reconcile the less determined catholics. The queen's power was declared to be that of supreme governor "as well in all spiritual and ecclesiastical things and causes as temporal", and was possibly meant to refer to matters of jurisdiction and not to any spiritual power conferred only by consecration. The precise nature of ecclesiastical supremacy was obscure to, and variously interpreted by, her councillors. The prayer book included a reference to the Real Presence in the prescribed form of the Eucharist, alongside the more protestant doctrine, and some express disavowals of catholic meaning in worship were removed. In these ways, Elizabeth expected to settle the religious differences by establishing a comprehensive church order, looking towards the two extremes, and yet founded on a definite middle course. Throughout her reign policy required that the more extreme protestants should be prevented from pushing the English reformation too fast and too far.

The history of English finances shows the same sense of responsibility and the same determination on the part of the queen to decide policy in the last resort. It was largely due to her strong character in imposing restraints on the ambitious plans of her advisers and in compelling strict economies, not only in her household but also in the departments of state, that England, unlike most continental states, was not forced into bankruptcy. Sir Thomas Gresham restored the coinage and national credit, and the Earl of Winchester reformed the financial administration, in the early years of her reign. Burleigh gave constant attention to financial detail and constant support to the queen's prudent conservation of her resources, but it was her own steady purpose to use her means for the best diplomatic returns which built up English power. It was only done by a continuous struggle on her part against the careless ways of her own servants, and the high demands of her allies.

Her achievement was all the more remarkable because the revenue at her own disposal was barely sufficient to meet the normal expenditure of peace time. Any emergency or campaign abroad led to considerable indebtedness on her part, as in her first years when the cost of meeting her sister's debts, of intervening in Scotland and of a French campaign amounted to more than three times the annual revenue. Her ordinary revenue was derived from crown lands, the customs, feudal incidents, the first fruits of benefices and the fines imposed in her courts of justice. Parliament was expected to grant extraordinary taxation for purposes of war and defence, but even in the years of war with Spain after 1588 the queen was forced to sell some £800,000 of crown lands to meet the very heavy expenses of subsidizing her protestant allies in France and the Netherlands, to carry on a naval war with Spain and to conduct a campaign in Ireland. During the thirty years prior to the Armada, the parliamentary grant averaged no more than £50,000 annually.

Throughout her reign, Elizabeth decided the main points of policy, trusting that the success which she gained would justify her in the eyes of her subjects. In the time of doubt and uncertainty preceding the actual outbreak of war, when strong minds urged a forward policy and a trial of strength, and the country was by no means united in its aims, it was her personality which gave the opportunity for moderate opinion to grow in favour of measures most likely to reconcile the people and to restore a positive sentiment of national unity. Her success depended on her power to prescribe and enforce a programme in which diplomatic, religious, military and financial questions were settled in terms of their interaction.

The results of her leadership were to be seen in the extraordinary display of enterprise and experiment in so many aspects of the nation's life, as if with returning strength and confidence the energies of the people were released from the burdens of fear and frustration of the middle of the century.

It was a time of economic recovery, and the government aimed at encouraging it by a variety of regulations and methods, taken in consultation with, or under pressure of, the interests directly concerned, but not without due care of wider interests, both of the people and of the commonwealth.

Burleigh aimed at giving substance to Gresham's hope of making Elizabeth' "a prince of power" by promoting England's self-sufficiency as far as nature permitted. In his hands mercantilism took shape. The balance of trade was to be made favourable to England, and the accumulation of capital was to make possible the establishment of new industries or the expansion of old ones necessary to increase national power. The use of foreign commodities was to be limited to such as were essential to national interests. The resources of the country were to be developed. New markets were to be discovered and old ones were to be protected.

The emphasis was on enterprise, invention and discovery, allied to a careful husbanding of resources and regulation of their use. Individuals and companies were to be induced to make the most of their opportunities, especially to make the best of the bad business conditions abroad. In one way, the unrest and strife in western Europe was an advantage by driving foreign capital and craftsmen to settle in England. The government did much to further this movement. In another way, the disruption of markets and the dangers to peaceful trading drove English merchants to search for markets in more peaceful areas.

The stability of the country, the application of a common policy according to the interests of the whole country, and its treatment as one economic unit greatly encouraged the tendencies to growth. Government regulation was not, in general, vexatious, and much of it could be evaded under the conditions of English administration. By the Statute of Artificers, 1563, the government attempted to arrest the decay of the corporate towns by insisting on apprenticeship in certain trades within the structure of the craft guilds. It also meant to aid agriculture by compelling other town workers to assist in the harvest. Wages were to be assessed with reference to conditions in different parts of the country and to suit times of scarcity as well as of plenty. Another act of 1563 limited the enclosure of land for pasture and even attempted to force owners to return to tillage if their lands had been ploughed for a period of four years since 1558. This act was repealed in 1593 but poor harvests in the succeeding years led the government to new legislation to prevent depopulation by enclosing for pasturage.

The most important legislation for social stability was the series of acts instituting measures to relieve the lot of the unfortunate, young or old, to provide work for the workless and to deal with the sturdy beggar. The seriousness of the problem led by stages to the comprehensive measure of 1598, differentiating between the three categories, prescribing measures according to their needs, work for the able-bodied in workhouses, apprenticeship for the children, and correction for the rogue. The justices of the peace had to appoint overseers of the poor in each parish and to assess all householders for a compulsory rate. By these measures the worst effects of the social changes were in some degree corrected, although the government proved unable to compel comformity to its strict pattern of ordered economic progress.

What impressed foreign observers was the interest in trade and industry. Sometimes it was a favourable impression as with Sir Thomas Craig, who recognized the English "faculty of commercial organization" and its resources of capital as superior to Scottish; sometimes it was unfavourable, as with Mendoza, the Spanish ambassador, who despised the English because "profit to them was like nutriment to savage beasts". The preoccupation with industry, however small its part in the national economy, was a feature of the reign. New inventions and new techniques, often acquired from abroad, produced in the last decades of the century a great advance in the relatively backward condition of English manufactures.

The metal industries, in particular brass, now introduced, and iron and copper were rapidly expanding. Guns were exported to the Continent. Search was made for ore deposits, and mining was assisted by new inventions, such as boring rods. There was a great demand for coal, stimulated by a growing shortage of timber, and it began to be used for making salt and bricks, as well as for producing steel from iron. New pits were sunk in areas where water—and therefore, cheap—transport was available. The Tyne coal trade by sea with the south showed a great increase. Machinery was used for draining the mines. Here are the beginnings of English heavy industry. Much of its development was due to enterprising individuals, many of whom gained substantial profits, and to investment by owners and yeomen, merchants and gentry, catholic and protestant.

Many other industries were set up as very small concerns, but the native cloth manufacture, enlarged by new kinds of cloth brought in by foreign immigrants, remained the principal export and the most important industry. It was moving away from the corporate towns, with their severe restrictions upon freedom of manufacture, to the country, and especially to the north, where cheap goods for the people became the foundation of a growing prosperity, and to the west, which concentrated on the older kinds of cloth. The organization of the industry showed considerable specialization. The clothiers became the organizing agents, planning the supply of raw materials and the disposal of the cloth, and providing credit to many small manufacturers, often working in their own cottages. Many clothiers were small masters; others were great employers. The export of cloth, which was especially encouraged by government measures in preference to the export of wool, was at last wrested from the Hanse towns by the Merchant Adventurers, whose monopoly led to such an expansion of trade by the end of the century and to such great prosperity that a determined attack was made upon the company.

Out of this greater economic activity came the three-pronged push into the remoter parts of the world. First, and in the long run the most important, was the development of trading companies. The Muscovy Company, founded in 1555, traded with the far north of Russia, and in time developed for some years an overland trade with Persia. The Eastland Company (1579) aimed at dominating Baltic trade. More important was the Levant Company (1581) which used the Mediterranean to supply more cheaply eastern goods obtained through Turkey. In 1600 the East India Company began to trade directly with

India. Although the risks of trade were great, the companies managed to make a profit. Secondly, the middle years of the reign saw notable, but fruitless attempts to discover ways into the Pacific by a north-east, and then a north-west, passage; and equally ill-fated attempts to establish trading stations in Newfoundland and Virginia. The merchants lost hope of profits and directed their efforts in other directions. The third way was the spectacular forcing of the King of Spain's American seas, the opening up of the Pacific by Drake, and the seizure of Spanish treasure. The unofficial war with Spain developed naval strength—a greater asset to England than the immediate profits of buccaneering.

Economic progress was closely connected with changes in society, changes so momentous that the Elizabethan order barely managed to contain them. The developments of at least two centuries came to dominate English society in the closing decades of the sixteenth century, and laid down its pattern for at least the two following centuries. The rise of the gentry to a position of local pre-eminence and leadership had begun before the end of the middle ages, and had become still more evident during the earlier agricultural and estate improvements of the sixteenth century. Landowners who were successful in these improvements built up enough capital from the surplus of the returns of the land to take advantage of Henry VIII's confiscation of church lands. The land yielded good returns to the improver.

Besides using his profits for further improvement, and to consolidate or enlarge his properties, he frequently shared in the economic activities of Elizabeth's reign, mining ore or coal, setting up iron works, making salt, always making the most of his resources. It was the enterprising who survived, the less adaptable succumbing to the great competition for land. There was a surprising amount of transference of land as families rose or fell. Successful members of the professional and official classes bought estates, but merchants who did so were exceptional in the sixteenth century. The towns, apart from London, were less important and merchants were socially inferior. They were still content with town life and their trading concerns.

The importance of estate management and capital investment in the growth of the country gentry was shown more strikingly in the fortunes of the nobility. The more old-fashioned failed to share in the growing wealth of the country, and tended to decay, but those who were ready to look after their estates, to adopt the same attitude as the gentry and to plan in terms of economic advantage held their place in the new order. The same forces were at work among the lower ranks of landed society, and, again, the improvers, provided that their security of tenure ensured to them the fruits of their efforts, built up their resources and some even became established as gentry. Others remained yeomen, no aspirants for county status, but bent on solid progress, and sometimes rivalling their betters in wealth. The yeoman knew his place, but he also knew his work and was prudent and painstaking in his search for profit, bearing in mind his posterity and treating his property as a family enterprise to be added to and developed by his shrewd descendants. There was considerable inequality among the lesser landholders, widespread bidding for holdings, and steadily increasing opportunities as the century advanced for the more enterprising as those on the margins of subsistence farming were squeezed out of their holdings.

Elizabethan society, then, was determined by the position of the gentry. They were entrenched in their localities, predominant in their counties, and beginning to supply national leaders in many fields. Their interests were related to their property and therefore held tenaciously and continuously. They were already in a position of considerable independence, not easily to be undermined, and attached to the laws—the common law—which gave them security in their possessions and protected their legitimate use. They were a litigious, aggressive and competitive class. There was as great a struggle to acquire land among them as in the lower classes. Marriage was an important method. The matrimonial alliances of the gentry were to play an important part in later politics. These connections became widespread and were bonds of peculiar toughness, giving support to their members, and offering the means of further prosperity or advancement.

Competition for favours, privileges and offices led to the competition of such connections, and to a clientele grouped around rival leaders. It was becoming a matter of local importance whether one group or another filled local offices and controlled local administration. Feuds were liable to divide the gentry: faction spread through society. Politics was a matter of prestige, of the local standing and influence of a family, and permeated all ranks of landed society. Tenants had no option but to support their landlords, and their relatives had little more. Influence over neighbouring towns was a matter of prestige to the gentry and also of importance to the towns because of advantages which could be made available or denied. The pressure behind these loose connections often came from below, from those who desired to gain or to hold local esteem, to be more illustrious than their rivals, and to be courted by their neighbours. Their leaders had to try to satisfy such aspirations. Fortunately for England the Tudors had taught the gentry that faction must work by influencing the administration and not by defying the state.

Tudor administration depended very largely upon the local justices of the peace, meeting in the quarter-sessions of the counties or by special commissions or sessions as new needs arose. It was in the quarter-sessions that their main judicial work was done. The traditional forms of local jurisdiction were derived from the self-governing communities of the middle ages, and those responsible for their working were limited only by the common law. They were not the mere servants of the crown. Under the Tudors the justices of the peace were made responsible for much administration under the new statutes and received powers to act by ones or twos, and in more convenient ways than quarter-session These new powers were exercised under the constant supervision of the king's councils. After the Reformation the parish gradually became the unit of secular administration, and its officials provided the justices with the means of continuous control. The tasks increasingly given to the justices were extremely varied and reflected the increasing functions of the state, in religion, economic regulation, with regard to the poor and the prevention of disorder. The justices of the peace were the means by which governmental programmes and policies were given reality in daily activity, and built up county by county the commonwealth of the nation. The sheriff's importance was declining, and the

Lord Lieutenants, a Tudor creation, existed for more specific purposes, primarily of defence.

All these offices were usually filled by the rural gentry. The central government had no alternative but to rely on their co-operation. There was no separate organization of officials, paid by the crown, obedient to its instructions, and empowered to override local opinion, just as there was no effective military power at the disposal of the crown. England's geographical position, the achievements of naval warfare and the success of the queen's diplomacy removed the necessity of a standing army. The closing of England's "back door", the frontier with Scotland, was of great importance in that respect.

The gentry were thus free to expand and to take advantage of their local indispensability. Not only did they supply voluntary and unpaid service but in their hands was the local assessment of parliamentary grants, and they were reluctant to lay too heavy a burden on themselves. For these reasons Elizabeth's government depended on prestige and persuasion. It is true that a strict control was exercised by the central government, and that justices of the peace were summoned before the council to answer for dilatory or negligent execution of their duties, but these measures were possible only by a general acceptance of the government's policy or by that considerable degree of deference to the government itself, which the queen was careful to preserve.

The council and its offshoots, Star Chamber and the councils of the north and of Wales, were the central organs of the central government, exercising constant control throughout the realm; over all persons irrespective of their powers and positions, concerned with all interests in all parts, taking account of all issues affecting the general interest. The council met the needs of more modern government and was suited to the newer functions of government. Above all it ensured that effective regulation of lesser agencies of government which was the condition of modern government. It settled disputes as to jurisdiction of courts and offices. The crown's prerogative was exercised through the council's, organized for this purpose on lines very different from the common law, with its protracted, formal and traditional procedures. The judicial powers of the council were exercised in public in Star Chamber, and the informal procedure, resting on written depositions and sometimes verbal confessions, allowed the judges, unhampered by juries, to give justice expeditiously. All classes were free to appeal to it for justice.

In the queen's time it was still a popular court. Already, however, the council of the north was exciting the resentment of the gentry, who, freed by its activity from aristocratic pressure and lawless ways, were anxious to take over the more normal methods of administration, now possible. The implied limits upon these councils was a political one—that their services were useful—and so long as there was no general sense of a difference between crown and subjects as to the interpretation of the ends of the state which the councils served, there was little need to attack their powers. But their purpose and large powers were associated with a new conception of the state akin, even if at several removes, to continental development.

The queen's council was her creature. She chose its members partly for their ability, partly for their importance in the country. They were identified with factions, and the queen "ruled much by faction and parties". In 1569 there was the clash of Burleigh and Norfolk, the leader of the older aristocracy, in alliance with Leicester; in the years before the Armada, it was the struggle of Burleigh against Leicester and Walsingham until Leicester overplayed his hand in the Netherlands and gave Burleigh the chance to bring supporters into the council; in the final years of the reign it was the tragic contest of Cecil and Essex. The queen played one against the other, committed herself to none, and retained her independence. It was to her advantage to have the factions competing at the council table, intriguing, manœuvring, organizing pressure to gain her support. At that table were laid bare the political realities, the conflict of interests, in the country, and she was able to estimate their strength, to influence them, and to discover the limits by which her policy had to be determined. She was as great a politician as she was a diplomatist.

It was in parliament that those responsible for central government met those responsible for local administration. The privy councillors sitting in the Commons were its leaders since

THE TUDOR COMMONWEALTH

they had knowledge and experience greater than the majority of members, who were local men, unknown to each other, unaccustomed to co-operate, and only meeting for infrequent and brief parliamentary sessions. They included few speakers of the same powers of argument and persuasion as were most of the councillors. Most of the bills concerned with public affairs came before the House after careful consideration by the government.

The initiative in the conduct of business lay with the government. It was as well: for the Commons were unfitted by composition and organization and function to decide policy and to direct government. Its function was negative—to present complaints, to convey local opinion, to criticize on the basis of local knowledge, and to veto government proposals. It was a collection of local celebrities, most of them, contrary to law, of the gentry, for all but a small minority of the boroughs returned the nominees of their patrons and protectors.

With the increase in the number of boroughs represented, under pressure of the gentry and not to enable the crown to dominate the Commons, more of the gentry became members and for longer periods. There was a fair proportion of members who sat in most of Elizabeth's parliaments, with the result that the Commons slowly developed a tradition and a procedure which added to its political importance. Committee work increased and bills were more fully debated. It was noted on occasion that the government position was sometimes modified in the course of debate to conciliate opponents.

It was important for the growth of the Commons' activities that the gentry were over-represented. Their local experience and position, and their social connections made the Commons less docile than if burgesses had predominated, and gave it a common character capable of developing later into a corporate tradition. Narrow as was the attitude of the gentry, it was not so tied to the protection of specific interests as was that of the towns. By 1603 the feud of Essex and Cecil, carried into parliamentary elections, was giving a political character to the earlier social significance of representation. Cecil initiated the process of managing borough elections by obtaining from their patrons the acceptance of his nominations. It brought in a systematic and centrally controlled political patronage, intended to secure power in the Commons, instead of a social and local patronage.

All Elizabethan parliaments were difficult to manage, and called for all the queen's ability to carry her policy by mingling threats and coercion with appeals to her success and to her popularity. The fractiousness of parliamentary critics was quelled by the outcome of a policy which won popular acceptance by its success, and parliamentary gratitude by its concessions. The queen insisted that it was not her intention to "break your liberties . . . but to stay you before you fell into the ditch" of an impetuous policy about the succession. After her virtual defeat over monopolies in her last parliament, she could still thank the Commons for their intervention by which she escaped falling "into the lap of an error, only for lack of true information".

Though troublesome, parliament was loyal: indeed, its loyalty led to much of the friction. In the critical issues of her marriage and succession, of puritanism and war, critical because the destiny of England seemed to be involved, the critics were as anxious as the queen. Their proposals were based on a simplification of the problems but sprang from their zeal for the safety of the kingdom. Their political immaturity was revealed in the financial debates of the last parliament. Willing to press a strong policy on the queen, parliament was reluctant to meet the necessary cost. That reluctance sprang from the ancient suspicion of the crown, and continued until the executive was answerable to parliament. Meanwhile, policy without provision put the Commons in a false position—that of an irresponsible assembly—and unavoidable until it first thought in terms of, and then assumed, the final responsibility for all government. In its sixteenth century form, government had attained its greatest efficiency under Queen Elizabeth, but the increase of its services and the modernizing of the state depended on the co-operation of the gentry, especially financial co-operation in the Commons. Those who valued efficiency inclined toward the prerogative rather than to trust the Commons.

The most vigorous expression of parliamentary opinion

emerged when the puritans challenged Elizabeth's church settlement. The Commons in general favoured the puritan desire for further religious reform and pressed upon the queen's prerogative. The puritan leaders recognized that their programme had to tarry for the co-operation of the civil magistrate, and sought to overcome the queen's obstinate insistence that the government of the church was solely a matter of royal prerogative, by the protests and pressure of the Commons.

The puritan ideal led the Commons to develop an alternative policy to the queen's and to prescribe the course of her government. Naturally she was but confirmed in her conviction that puritanism involved a political issue, and was fixed in her determination to prevent "every man according to his own censure to make a doom of the validity and privity of his prince's government" or "to frame a form of religion or a state of government"; absurdities "which no king fit for his state" would suffer. The opinions uttered in the Commons, especially by Wentworth, were shocking to the House itself. On this issue the queen was unyieldingly conservative. The puritans, desperately aggressive, went too far in the logical exposition of their programme, and were defeated, but the alliance of crown and gentry was shaken.

It is not easy to see what else the queen could have done without surrendering the whole basis of her government. There was a logic in the puritan platform which meant increasing interference by the Commons and increasing subjection of the lay magistrate to the law of God championed by the puritan House. It was implicit that the queen must conform in religious fundamentals and order her government in accordance with them. To agree must have undermined her whole policy, and reversed the crown's relation to the Commons. A sermon before the queen made the point clearly. "And yet you, in the meanwhile that all these whoredoms are committed, you at whose hands God will require it, you sit still and are careless, let men do as they list. It toucheth not, belike your Commonwealth, and therefore you are so well contented to let all alone."

To the puritan, the Reformation was the reform of man, not only of an ecclesiastical institution, and therefore penetrated to the roots of all society. If the queen had no choice but to resist such a philosophy of society, it was none the less politically a fateful step. For one thing it marked off an irreconcilable body and made a division in the Commonwealth. For another it threatened the co-operation of crown and gentry by forcing the puritan Commons to utter claims which echoed throughout the seventeenth century sessions of parliament. Finally, it identified crown and prerogative with the maintenance of an episcopacy, which was at first hard put to it to justify itself on grounds other than the royal supremacy, and when it did, had to revive the old doctrine of its divine right.

The court of High Commission set up to restore ecclesiastical discipline was really a royal instrument, and the means of checking puritan aggression in the church. But the common lawyers were beginning to challenge its prerogative power, possibly because the crown's prerogative in ecclesiastical affairs was exercised without any partner, unlike its use in civil concerns. The fact that local government rested with the gentry meant that puritan gentry were unlikely to enforce the laws against puritans. Having many influential sympathisers, they were able to survive and to trouble her successor's son.

The queen's policy toward the church was singularly inflexible: nothing ever changed her attitude to the puritans. She attempted no compromise, made no advance beyond the medieval uniformity and conformity of society and thwarted Bancroft's compromise with the catholics. She insisted on the royal supremacy and episcopacy because bishops were essential to her conception of the monarchy. She was committed to a particular conception of her office which she would not modify in the church, where there was no ecclesiastical parliament, no General Assembly. Her church was her bulwark.

This inflexible position was not due to religious but to political reasons, and the question arises whether she had not made a political miscalculation. It is not a question of whether she or the puritans were right, but of the political wisdom of a policy which strained the alliance of crown and gentry, which forced the puritans to work through the House of Commons, partly for want of a General Assembly, and which magnified the royal supremacy and therefore prerogative government. The alienation of the puritans, defeated but not conforming, strained the Elizabethan system of governing with the co-operation of the gentry and foreshadowed Stewart government by part of the gentry over the rest. Elizabeth, however, was too patriotic and too much of a statesman merely to have sought a temporary solution at the expense of her successor.

During Elizabeth's long reign there emerged the great differences in politics and religion which were to become still sharper in the next century, when opposition to the crown became popular and uncompromising. Until 1603 there was little desire for careful definition of the issues and less concern with the principles at stake. Men were dealing with practical grievances with the help of the slowly changing traditional thought. A few extremists insisted on the difference of principle but most of the minorities were content to defend themselves by less consistent and more temporizing policies. Catholics and puritans avoided drawing the logical conclusions of their positions. Still truer is it that the "Anglican" attitude was practical and instinctive, and formulated late in the reign when events had determined its general outline and success had justified what principles it had.

There was general reluctance to study the different points of view as clear-cut alternatives. Elizabeth's success in warding off civil war had reduced the heroic temper and made way for a more accommodating frame of mind. It is significant that there was no great book of political theory and little political inquiry before the last phase of an age of great endeavour and achievement. It was not for lack of challenging questions, nor for want of ability, but because there seemed no feasible alternative to the traditional working of the constitution, in which parliament played a subordinate, though at times necessary, part.

England was generally understood to be a commonwealth: "a society or common doing of a multitude of free men collected together and united by common concord and covenants among themselves, for the conservation of themselves as well in peace as in warre". Ideas derived from feudal ranks and liberties were extended to all free men and lost their narrow meanings. The Commonwealth was held together by obedience to a law defining and securing the rights and duties of each according to his station, and which was not made or unmade according to the will of men. For that reason law was generally regarded as fundamental, existing before the agencies by which it was executed and giving to them their authority, though also prescribing their duties. Nobody was yet ready to claim that something was right simply because of a power to enforce it. What was right and just did not arise from any human will, and it was only right that men should recognize and declare what they saw to be right and just.

There was some difference of opinion as to what this fundamental law was. By the lawyers it was often interpreted as the customs of the realm consolidated in the common law and requiring long study and experience for its formulation and application. Ordinary reason was inadequate. To the Calvinist the Scriptural law of God lay behind all human law. To Hooker, human reason was as much God's way of instructing man in justice as the Scriptures. No party claimed freedom from the law: each contented itself with arguing that the fundamental law, the true law, which was to be applied throughout the land expressed the party's programme and clothed it with a nation-wide authority. There was, therefore, no idea of sovereignty, of a supreme and unlimited power whose will was law, and authorized to enforce obedience to it. There was indeed, scarcely any idea of making law; only of applying and declaring it according to new conditions and issues, and in line with the body of existing law.

Law was given in many courts but the supreme court was that of parliament, higher than any other court, and from which no appeal could be made. Parliament was itself under the law; it was supreme not in regard of the law, but of all other courts in the land. Its judicial and legislative functions were only beginning to be separated in consequence of the religious changes which it had sanctioned under the Tudors. The authority of parliament—"its high, absolute and authenticall power"—belonged to it as representing the king and three estates, the great corporation or body politic of the kingdom. "For every Englishman is entended there to be present ... from the prince to the lowest person. And the consent of the Parliament is taken to be every man's consent."

In the Tudor Commonwealth, king and parliament were joint organs with powers regulated and protected by the law. The monarchy was an organ and not the master, and ruled by laws which, while limiting it, equally confirmed its powers. Its prerogative, if left vague, was the product of the laws. Certain matters were the king's alone and were not to be invaded by any act of parliament. He was free to act as he pleased in a large number of cases and was granted an absolute discretion in some kinds of acts. But the extent and exercise of the prerogative depended on legal limitations which the courts were to interpret. The ideal was still seen as a mixed government of joint organs, ordered under the law, mutually dependent, and embodying the consent of the whole body politic. Such an ideal required the co-operation of the organs. As that co-operation became less possible in the seventeenth century, as king and parliament became opposed, precedents assuming the joint activity of both and only consistent when joint activity was normal, proved unable to govern their relations as opponents.

It was then that the question of sovereignty became acute and led to the formulation of the parliamentary claim to legislative sovereignty. But in the balanced Tudor polity, with large and vague powers of king, council, parliament and law, and together ordering the commonwealth, all could be seen as somehow, if obscurely, subject to the king in parliament, a convenient formula assuming more than it explained. The king's politic capacity, his inseparable prerogative, the council's power to issue proclamations and to raise money, his powers in relation to parliament, were accepted as necessary to the crown so long as it was a part of the commonwealth and agreed with the joint supremacy of king in parliament.

The English Reformation had completed the evolution of the commonwealth by furthering the national ideal of independence of any external jurisdiction, and of the subjection of all its members, clergy and laity, to its law. English sentiment was strongly anti-clerical and strongly nationalist. The supremacy of the crown in the church became the symbol of anti-clerical nationalism. The church was not a separate and independent organization, governed by rules and institutions different from those of the state. Church and state were aspects of the same commonwealth and bound together by a common way of life. Members of the one were members of the other. Christians were citizens. Political and ecclesiastical authority ruled the same persons and directed them by complementary methods to the same end.

In the autonomous commonwealth there seemed no room for any other government, and no need of it. If, as was assumed in England, the essentials of the true religion were accepted, if the purely religious ordinances were regulated by the clergy, and if the spiritual power guided christians by spiritual means, that was all that religion required. There was no need of government in the church apart from the government of the commonwealth. Indeed, there was but one source of government—the commonwealth itself. If the church was to be endowed with power to make laws, to enforce discipline and to impose uniformity, it was because the commonwealth agreed and granted that power; because the body of believing citizens gave the sanction of law, of coercion and of power in ecclesiastical matters in the same way as in civil matters—through the supreme authority representing the commonwealth. The spiritual power of the church, its proper power, knew nothing of law and coercion and government. It was for the commonwealth to decide whether to support the church with such means, and to regulate their use.

In an age when church and state were not separable, when lay feeling, quickened by the Renaissance, was strong and influenced royal counsels, it was not mere Caesaro-papism for the supreme power to insist that the governmental means used to establish the church were not to erect an independent clerical power, using these means over the laity without any accountability to it, without respect of its convictions, though granted with its agreement by the supreme governor of the commonwealth. Moreover, Queen Elizabeth might fairly be regarded as the representative of the great body of laity relatively indifferent to forms of church government; of the nation as against the sect striving to raise the nation to its own spiritual levels.

Under sixteenth century conditions the victory of either side was bound to imply tyranny to the loser. To subordinate the living church of Christ to the standards of society at large was an affront to the Christian conscience. Even Archbishop Grindal made a vigorous protest to the queen when she instructed him to limit the preaching ministry which puritanism zealously promoted. "I am forced with all humility, and yet plainly, to profess that I cannot with safe conscience and without offence to the majesty of God, give my assent to the suppressing of the said exercises." He warned her equally plainly that "when you deal in matters of faith and religion or matters which touch the church of Christ, which is his spouse ... you would not use to pronounce so resolutely and peremptorily *quasi ex auctoritate*, as ye may do in civil and extern matters".

It was also true that the application of principles valid enough for the members of what was really a voluntary society to a whole community by political machinery and methods would cause offence to many consciences. To defend the church as expressing the free consciences of willing members against the lay authority was indeed to defend the spiritual realm, but equally the queen was defending the spirit when she resisted the aggressive designs of puritanism to transform a voluntary society into a national. The issue would have been clearer had Elizabethan England been a political democracy. Puritanism in such a case would not have accepted a democratic settlement of the church. Elizabeth was probably more representative of national sentiment than the puritans, but her defence of the laity necessarily forced her to measures dangerously near to a usurpation of spiritual functions.

It was in the last half of the reign that Whitgift and Hooker developed in its clearest forms the conception of the commonwealth, of which the church was one aspect. They rejected the claim that the ends of the church were different from those of the commonwealth, as if it existed only for temporal and material ends. They denied that the Scriptures laid down any system of church government, and they insisted that the puritan disagreed only upon matters which were indifferent and not essential to christianity.

Alongside this argument, there was beginning another which was to mark a new and more bitter stage in the religious conflict. After 1585 Bishop Bancroft defended episcopacy on the ground of divine right which turned the Elizabethan bishop, a minister with a civil commission, into a successor of the Apostles by whom episcopacy had been instituted. The puritans had suspicions of the first and open hostility to the second. But the new defence of bishops marks the decay of the conception of the commonwealth, since a theory of a *jure divino* episcopacy was radically opposed to the theory of royal supremacy, as Sir Francis Knollys argued in his letter to Burleigh.

It was the growth of puritanism which really denied Hooker's great statement of a dying ideal. The commonwealth of believers was split, and the puritans held a fundamentally opposed conception of the church and of the state. The ends of the church were distinct from those of the state; there was a presbyterian system of church government in the Scriptures, with laws and institutions separate from civil authority; and such matters as the use of the surplice, of the ring in marriage and of the cross in baptism were not matters of indifference to the true religion.

The separation of the church was essential to its independence, and its independence was essential for the rule of the godly minority according to the law of God. The church tended to be identified with the courts of office-bearers. In these courts the position of the laity might be transposed, for none, not even the queen, was exempted from divine law and excommunication, and the lay officers were men called on grounds other than those by which civil offices were held. In the church, the laity was ordered in a way very different from its civil relations of one to another, and therefore no fundamental bond or community could exist between the laity as members of the church and as members of the state. Not only were their two capacities different, but also their status.

The puritans, strictly speaking, believed in the national church and held that the Church of England was sufficiently pure for it to be a sin to separate from it. Their aim was to reform that church and to purge it of its idolatrous relics. No deviation in doctrine or discipline and no separation from the church were to be permitted. Their conception, first, of the church and, then, of the national church, gave to the puritan theory of the relation of church and state its peculiar form. For though separated and differently organized, the members of the both were the same persons and the problems with which both were concerned were the same social difficulties. The lay officers of the church were to work according to their secular position in the state to ensure its conformity to God's law. Moreover, the church was to influence all civil officers as members of the church, if necessary by excommunication. In the puritan ideal the civil state would function according to the law of God, and in harmony with the church, and therefore civil power would tend to fall to the same lay hands as were prominent in the church. The pattern of civil government would conform to an ecclesiastical model.

In attacking the Anglican commonwealth, the puritans proposed a system just as intimate, though weighted in favour of the church. The royal supremacy was to enforce the law of God and to uphold the church. Such dreams remained dreams while Elizabeth ruled. None of the Elizabethan puritans taught any doctrine of resistance although the queen resisted their programme. Denied official help, they were forced to rely on the difficulty of the government to compel the strict and constant administration of the laws against puritans, and upon their own power to attract congregations. They had to adopt the methods of persuasion, of argument and witness by example, but this was to open the way to applications and extensions of their principles which were later to overthrow the presbyterian bid to dominate England.

The English puritans were never radicals. They fought bitterly the destructive tenets of the Congregationalists who first began to separate from the Church of England in Elizabeth's reign. Their numbers were very small and their members mainly came from the lower ranks of society; but their obscurity did not diminish the challenge of their principles to the society in which they maintained a precarious existence. It was a challenge which was ever ready to take new forms as "the spirit" brooding over the Scriptures arrived at further enlightenment. John Smyth, one of the leaders in the separated church, acknowledged that he had changed his views "and shall be ready still to change for the better". Here was expressed the full sense of the ultimate responsibility of the individual conscience which ended in the astounding outburst of religious sects after 1645. The nature of the new church organization prevented any restriction of this individual responsibility since the congregational church rested on the co-operation of its members. Divisions and secessions were as many as there were leaders with differing doctrines and ability to win followers. There was even the strange spectacle of rival leaders excommunicating each other. There were many variations of worship and government even among the Congregationalists proper, but they were usually united on certain basic principles.

It was their conception of the church which was fundamental. It was for them a voluntary society of the laity, who shared the same religious experience of being called by God and who bound themselves by a church-covenant to maintain a common witness and order. None were members without this personal experience and personal profession of willingness to live together according to the spirit, and no church could exist without such members.

It was, therefore, the body of true believers, the "willing sort", who were the church: no other relation constituted a church and no other body could act in the place of the body of true believers. Only the "particular" church of small numbers fulfilled these conditions. No parish church, no "representative" church (i.e. of delegates or officers) and no national church was a real church but mere human tyrannies over the spirit. It was only in the congregation that the spirit dwelt and worked, and the congregation was unable to abandon or to delegate the power of the spirit. No other church or church agency was able to interfere even in a case of backsliding save by recreating the first condition of the fallen church in its purity and power, and therewith its original power to order its own affairs.

The essence of Congregationalism was this vital religious community for which there was no substitute and without which there was no church. In each congregation there was a self-sufficiency of power and each was self-governing. The relations between the individual churches were one of criticism, encouragement and support, but not of jurisdiction and authority.

The predominance of the laity was equally seen in the Congregational principle of lay-preaching and lay-participation in the communion service of the Last Supper. Barrow, executed in 1593, denounced pulpits as limiting the congregation to the gifts of one man. The gift of prophecy for Barrow belonged to "the whole church and none of them ought to be shut out". Prayer was to be made by all according to their gifts. "Is not this presumptuous to undertake to teach the Spirit of God, and to take away his office," he asks of the Liturgy. The officers of the church did not differ in kind from the church-member who appointed and removed them.

The Congregationalists regarded themselves as the godly or "choice professors" of the puritans but rejected the puritan national church, and the rule of the godly in it by means of civil compulsion over the ungodly. Barrow reproached the puritans with having "*the whole land* to be '*the church*' ", by way of a political reformation to "have all redressed in one day" instead of reforming by "the word preached", and when "it hath wrought in their hearts true repentance and conversion". It was wrong to include all profane and ignorant men in the church, and then to direct against them the full force of ecclesiastical discipline. The puritans, moreover, set the clergy above the people. The new office of elder prevented the people from knowing and doing their duties in the church of Christ. The elders would be "the wealthiest, honest, simple men in the parish, that shall sit for cyphers by their pastors and meddle with nothing". The people would have nothing but "the smoaky, windy title of election" of their ministers.

The outcome of Congregationalism was the antipathy of church and state. The state was limited to civil transgressions, for its means and methods were not such as to bring about genuine conviction and therefore wholly distinct from those needed to establish the true church. There was no place for a royal supremacy. But this was the point of view of the Brownists rather than of Barrow, who laid upon rulers the duty to promote the true and to eradicate the false worship of God.

The exiled separatist congregation at Amsterdam declared in its Confession of 1596 that "it is the duty of princes and magistrates to suppress and root out by their authority all false ministries, voluntary religions and counterfeit worship of God, yea, to enforce all their subjects, whether ecclesiastical or civil to do their duties to God and men." Greenwood admitted that the ruler ought to compel infidels to hear the doctrine of the church.

In the petition of 1603 to James I, the Separatists called on the king to employ his lawful authority to root out antichristian worship, to confiscate popish livings and Jewish tithes in order that the church might be supported by the voluntary contributions of its members, and to remove the burden of civil affairs, such as marriages and burying the dead, from the officers of the church. To call upon the ruler to act in civil matters and to prevent false worship was not to admit any power in the true faith. The Separatists denied compulsion where grace alone was effective, not so much in the interest of individual unbelievers as in the interest of the church and its purity. They had not as yet any thought of toleration, but they did repudiate the puritan outward conformity of conduct and the Anglican outward conformity of worship.

CHAPTER III

THE CONSERVATIVE REVOLUTION

THE succession of James to the English throne made him the ruler of a people which not only had been welded into unity by the vigour of Tudor administration, but also was becoming increasingly conscious of its common interests and character. During Elizabeth's long reign the Tudor commonwealth was securely established upon the basis of co-operation of crown and people, and by a wise combination of governmental direction and social enterprise. If the queen commanded, she did so for the good of her subjects as she saw it, and in the light of her counsellors' opinions and popular convictions.

England in 1603 was a more integrated country than ever before. The machinery of government was no longer obstructed by the resources of feudal subjects or the separate jurisdiction of the church. Although regional differences survived, no part of the country escaped the regulating power of the central government. The duties of the government took on a national character, dealing with the needs of the whole people. Economic interests were a national concern, involving all classes and all areas, and calling for national regulation. The church and, through it, important aspects of opinion and thought, were determined in accordance with a nationalistic outlook. The government had been forced to assume responsibility at a national level for the adjustment and direction of the major activities of the people.

It was also evident by 1603 that the different spheres of government were more closely related than at the beginning of Elizabeth's reign. The responsibility for defence was related to religious and economic policies. Religious convictions necessarily affected social, economic and foreign policies. Clearly, the duty of the government to provide a unified administration, adequate to the needs of the people, required a general acknowledgment of the fact that the different interests were too closely connected to be dealt with by different authorities and in accordance with different policies.

The success of the Tudors in organizing a government able to undertake the centralized direction of the many social and economic interests within a national framework helped to evoke a sense of unity among the people in proportion as the sense of mutual dependence and a common interest became more pronounced. The people had become aware of its unity, of the importance of acting in common, and of the superior claim of the national interest. The close of Tudor rule saw the acknowledged triumph of a "public power" supreme over the different elements of society and authorized to secure the general interest of the people; but this development had aided the unification of the people and quickened its consciousness of its general interest.

The nature and organization of the public power were still uncertain in 1603 as was its relation to the general interest and public welfare, and the ways in which such interest and welfare were determined, but the Tudors had vindicated such a power and justified it by such interest and welfare. The important question for Stewart England in the seventeenth century was the precise relation between the government and the nation, and between the public power and public welfare. The constitutional struggles under the Stewarts were not an attempt to undo the work of the Tudors, but to discover the principles and the means by which the claims of the people and the responsibilities of government might be equitably adjusted.

Before Elizabeth's death, it was evident that the traditional ideas of the constitution no longer fitted the new situation. The power of the Crown had grown with the needs of the nation. Tudor government had rested upon the monarch's councils and their prerogative powers. An independent authority enabled the crown to decide policy and to put it into operation. The one great limitation upon the government was its inability to raise taxes necessary for the burdens of the new national government without the co-operation of parliament, and Elizabeth had barely managed to resist the pressure which the Commons were able to exercise through the power to refuse taxation. The tension between the government and parliament in her last years foreshadowed the difficulty of finding a solution of the political problems of governing the country in terms of the old constitution.

Questions of obedience and authority, of the powers and purposes of government, were still answered in accordance with medieval ideals, increasingly inadequate to meet the political needs of modern government. It was generally recognized that government was the duty of the monarch, and that monarchy, divinely sanctioned, possessed certain prerogatives peculiar to its place in the constitution. Appointments to high office were made by the monarch; it was for him to decide when to summon and to dissolve parliament; war and peace, foreign policy and military and economic regulation of the community for its defence were matters to be decided by him alone. It was granted that the king had a discretionary authority to promote the general welfare. Undisputed as these powers were, they were not treated in isolation from the rights of subjects. Just as the king had his prerogative, independent of his subjects, so had subjects their property and rights independent of the king and, therefore, limiting the sphere of independent royal action. Only by the consent of the subjects were their rights to be modified.

These two sets of rights—of government and property—were held apart and defended by the law. There was no sense of a real and permanent opposition between them; whenever a clash occurred, it was a question for the law to define the extent of government and of property. If the king had no power over subjects' rights, subjects had none over the king's rights, and both had to look to the law for the justification of their claims. Within the framework of the constitution each had an assured place.

It was not thought that the government and the subject were necessarily in conflict because, on the one hand, the king was presumed to fulfil his duties without endangering the normal activities of his subjects and, on the other hand, the adjustment of conflicting rights was possible under the overriding authority of law. Whenever a particularly intractable problem or novel issue warranted, the different interests meeting in parliament were able to clarify their respective rights and to adjust their rival claims. Statute law was a particularly solemn agreement as to what the law was and took account of the interests and required the consent of the king and his estates, without which the status of each remained as before.

Parliament, in which the king, the House of Lords and the House of Commons were essential parts, united the main competing interests of the community for the purposes of co-operative adjustment. The consent of each part was necessary thus providing a certain independence for each and a necessary opportunity to bargain with the other, without which lasting agreement was impossible. The necessity of obtaining consent also imposed a limit upon the independent action of any constituent part of parliament. The king, especially, was limited by the need of parliamentary consent to statute and to taxes. Considerable as was his exclusive prerogative in matters of government, he was unable to enlarge his sphere of independent action or to invade the separate areas of subjects' rights.

This traditional view of parliament explains the common conception of the English constitution as mixed or balanced, a conception influential throughout the seventeenth century. It was a political balance and not a balance of great organized interests in society. It was a balance between prerogative and rights: it was also a balance between the organs of parliament. The harmonious co-operation of parts with independent rights, essential to the commonwealth, required respect for such rights and consultation between their legal holders. The emphasis on balance made it difficult to see parliament as a sovereign law-making body, and the emphasis on rights seemed to deny the existence of any unified and absolute power, making law as it willed.

This constitutional doctrine no longer corresponded to political realities by 1603 and provided no solution to the critical problem of the times, that is, the formulation of policy. The unification of the state and integration of the country's interests transformed differences of outlook and disputes as to rights into issues of policy, which resisted settlement by appeal to law. The progress of the country broke down the separation between government and property, and upset the balance of the constitution. The political needs of government—law and order, defence and foreign relations, economic and ecclesiastical control—required a policy recognizing their interconnection and adjusting each one to the other. Administration and finance needed to be more closely adapted to the governmental system than was possible under the old constitution. In its turn, policy affected the subjects' interests more directly and more generally. Foreign policy was linked to religious convictions and economic interests were affected by administrative action. Parliamentary activity under Elizabeth had shown that subjects were seeking to shape policy indirectly by the power to refuse legislative and financial proposals.

Royal directions to parliament and parliamentary pressure on the crown indicated that the formulation of policy was of increasing importance, and that the balanced constitution was working imperfectly. Its defects became more obvious when co-operation became more difficult on account of differences of policy. Adjustment of rival claims to meet a new situation was less easy and the rival organs of government each holding firmly to their legal powers, impeded efficient government. In times of change the law was unsuited to preserve unity, and men's opinions of what was the law became of primary significance. The claim of efficient government influenced some statesmen after 1603. Government was a royal responsibility whether parliament co-operated or not. Other statesmen recognized the claims of parliament to share in the task of adjusting the rights of king and subjects to present needs of government, and defended parliamentary obstruction of the king as the only way to secure the recognition of that share.

In the period from 1603 to 1640, moderate opinion among royal and parliamentary supporters wished to preserve the proper place of king and parliament in a co-operative scheme which they believed still to be possible. A few extreme thinkers interpreted the general opinion in favour of greater unity in government to mean the need of a unified authority to decide an integrated policy. Some saw the king, others parliament, to be this authority. Seventeenth century England did not accept the logical simplicity of the extremists' thought: it limited the dispute to the *proper* powers of rival organs of government.

Scottish politics during these same years were less strongly influenced by the moderates' opinions, and it proved much more difficult than in England to gain support for a middle way by which the extremists were held in check. This was due in part to the ecclesiastical issue on which extremists readily divided and gained support. In England religious divisions were checked by the predominance of the constitutional issue, whereas in Scotland the actual weakness of parliament made the constitutional question academic. In part, however, the comparative weakness of the moderates was due to their dependence on royal patronage; both episcopalian and presbyterian moderate opinion were growing in strength under the shelter of James' favour and power.

James' reign after 1603 consolidated his earlier work in Scotland and he derived considerable help from his resources and prestige as King of England. He was secure in London from the crude control of violent factions and English ships were able to deploy his armed forces much more decisively against rebellious feudatories. The church had already lost much of its power over the king and his government. The greater part of James' success, however, was due to the support of the moderates in constitutional and ecclesiastical disputes who found in the king's policies a way of escape from the extreme tension of Scottish politics after the Reformation. Until his last years James was careful to nurse this growing, but by no means established, body of thought.

James' concern had been to achieve the well governed commonwealth, to promote security and prosperity and to encourage the integration of the country—in short, to carry through a Tudor policy in Scotland and to release it from medieval bonds. For these ends he had to assert the public power over all rivals and to revive its political primacy. It was largely due to his determination that the public power gained general acknowledgment and was not destroyed but taken over in the later days of revolution. It was in moderate circles that this policy was understood and supported.

Since it was by the king's initiative that the public power was asserted, it was inevitable that its organization took the form of personal government. James governed Scotland through a dependent privy council, which developed its functions and extended the range of its activities during the years of peaceful and orderly administration. It proved more efficient, once its authority was upheld, than feudal agencies, and royal government gained in popularity. Parliament was no rival, for it fell under royal influence. James used his prerogative of summoning and proroguing parliament to eliminate all meetings other than the opening meeting to select the Lords of the Articles and the final meeting in which their work was submitted for formal approval. The Lords of the Articles only were in continuous session, and all other members of parliament were forbidden to meet, even in private.

James sometimes nominated the Lords of the Articles, but obtained equally effective, although less public, control by reviving the pre-Reformation method in which the nobles chose the bishops and the bishops chose the nobles to serve as Lords of the Articles. All the nobles and bishops chose the representatives of the barons and burgesses, but after 1621 this was done by the nobles and bishops chosen as Lords of the Articles. Since the bishops were dependents of the king he was able to control the Lords of the Articles. Public business had to be introduced into parliament through them so that all proposals and criticism obnoxious to the king were easily suppressed.

The Lords of the Articles were the means of forcing the officially inspired programme through parliament. It was the privy council, by the end of the reign composed of officials, which prepared the measures to be submitted to parliament. Taxation was much lighter and rarer than in England. There was not the same tendency for parliament to interfere in policy on that account; although criticism grew at the end of the reign when taxation, caused largely by English policies of the king, became heavier. James found parliament useful enough to contrive its subordination to his will and to prevent its control by faction.

The restoration of episcopacy was intended to secure the king's influence in the church and in the kingdom. Political motives were the most important. Bishops were dependable servants in administration and in parliament, but it was also through them that James expected to end the presbyterian pressure on the king by controlling the General Assembly. He was cautious in carrying through the restoration, first breaking the extremist opposition, then obtaining an agreement between nobles and bishops, and by nominated ministers obtaining assent to perpetual moderators in each presbytery. In 1609 two courts of High Commission, later united, were set up by proclamation to decide all moral and religious offences. Finally in 1610 episcopal authority was sanctioned at the expense of the parity of presbyterian ministers.

James was cautious, too, in claiming only a "power innated and a special prerogative" to govern the external order of the church, and in defending episcopacy on grounds of convenience and not by divine right. His and their authority was "in things indifferent and not repugnant to the Word of God", that is, an authority supplementary to and permitted by the divine authority of the Word. This principle denied the fundamental claim of the extremists who held to presbytery by divine right, the only rightful authority in the church.

There was remarkably little opposition to the changes in church government, but the king's policy in 1617 to use the bishops to introduce some change in ritual, reluctantly accepted in 1618 in the Five Articles of Perth, began a sporadic resistance among the laity, now first taught the meaning of the king's authority in things indifferent and in the external government of the church. Ritual was not indifferent to the laity who began to give support to the presbyterian extremists. The king dropped other proposals of greater ecclesiastical uniformity with England although not before injuring the cause of the moderate party and its confidence in him without any real need.

James' work in Scotland had considerable success. The fear, echoed by conservative lawyers throughout the seventeenth century although repudiated by the bold Buchanan, tutor of James and teacher of resistance, if necessary, by private individuals to tyranny, that the Scots were unable to govern themselves, was relieved by the strength of James' rule. It had, however, a certain artificial character. James relied upon playing the various interests in the country against each other.

As King of England his work was less successful because he was faced by a very different political problem, but also because he relied upon balancing groups instead of putting himself at the head of moderate opinion.

The measure of his failure was his inability to reconcile his legal position as head of the government to the political facts of parliamentary power. He was rarely able to co-operate with his parliaments. His policies in religion, in foreign relations and in administration were opposed to policies expressed in parliament. His independent government, marred by extravagant and incompetent administration, produced parliamentary criticism of his policies, his ministers and his methods. Parliament strove to influence policy by refusing to agree to laws and taxes, without which the king's policy was unlikely to succeed.

James probably underestimated the resources of hostile parliaments but he was too shrewd not to see that the political issue was one of principle. He certainly acted as if he realized that any concession to parliament would sweep away the monarchical government which he had inherited from the Tudors. He was not prepared to surrender any of the rights of the crown held by his predecessors.

In his speeches to parliament, often lectures on constitutional law, he defended his interpretation of the relation of king and parliament. He admitted that England had its own fundamental laws, the duties of subjects were to be fulfilled according to the ancient form and order of the kingdom, and the king had no power to make laws or to tax without the advice of parliament. He acknowledged the common law as the protector of rights of property and of government and as able to extend royal rights more than any other law. He recognized the difference between "the general power of a King in Divinity and the settled and established state of this crowne and Kingdome". Ready to assert the duty of subjects to support the king, especially by taxes, he granted that parliament was to determine the time and amount of supply.

He learned from his councillors that "the king with his parliament here are absolute . . . in making or forming of any sort of Lawes", but he did not understand this absolute power to be a sovereign lawmaking power over all other powers in the commonwealth. The making of law was subordinate to its enforcement and interpretation. Since the executive was more important than the legislature, the king was at the least independent of parliament. To preserve the great body of law was more important than "heaping up infinite and confused numbers of Lawes".

To James the purpose of parliament was to bring together the local knowledge of members for the information and guidance of the king, who was to initiate legislative proposals. Parliament was no place for "every rash and harebrained fellow to propone new lawes of his owne invention". He criticized its independent leanings as ways of pushing private interests in the name of the public good but often to its detriment, and also the practice of its members of voicing general grievances popular with the people. The House of Commons was already a true political assembly and James had grounds for his criticism of the political activities, often representing group interests, of its members.

Parliament was entitled to voice a genuine grievance. In defining this power, James touched on an important issue. He held a genuine grievance to be the abuse of a law or its maladministration, and not what was lawfully done in accordance with a "settled law" which, being the work of parliament, was never a genuine grievance. For parliament to complain of laws properly administered was to abridge the king's power, and for the House of Commons to agitate for legislative changes was to admit the right of a part to challenge the work of the whole. If, then, the king with his parliament was absolute in law-making, the law and the rights of the king were unalterable and binding upon all the commonwealth, until the king, as well as the Houses agreed to amendment. James used the law-making power of king in parliament to limit the activities of the Commons.

Most royalists went no further than James. Rights of property were upheld by royalist judges and the share of parliament in law-making and in taxation was admitted by royalist publicists, but like James, they stressed the executive as independent of the legislature. The king's responsibility for government was to them a matter of law whether parliament co-operated or not. Parliament might refuse to change laws or to grant taxes, in which case the king might be hampered, but parliament had no right to encroach on the king's office. Accepting the unprecedented situation in which king and parliament were in more or less continual conflict, his lawyers sought to gain for the king's independent prerogative as much power as the law sanctioned, and to obtain formal and public acknowledgment of it in the courts. The king was the public representative of the kingdom although deprived of such powers as were shared with parliament, and not to be resisted without resisting the law itself. In the balanced constitution there was no legal means by which the king might coerce parliament but equally no provision for the coercion of the king by parliament.

The important question was the powers given by the law to the king, and his opponents fought a long and bitter struggle to define the law narrowly enough to prevent the possibility of the king governing the country legally without parliament. If he could circumvent the refusal of parliament to co-operate, the political point of that obstruction—indirectly to influence policy—was lost. Parliament lacked confidence in James I and Charles I, largely because each king resisted its encroachment on his authority. Nor was either markedly successful in his policy and so able to influence public opinion favourably.

The parliamentary opposition relied upon the rights of property as legally secured against the king's prerogative and as absolute against the king's claim to protect and promote the public interest. Property was not to be taken without the individual's consent except by the consent of parliament. The legal limits on the king's prerogative were stressed. Although the king's discretionary power in emergencies and his independent right to make appointments and control foreign affairs were still unquestioned, rights of property were absolute. In 1628 the Petition of Right set down the subjects' rights in absolute form, without any reference to the royal prerogative, as their legal rights according to the Common law. The country was in general united for the protection of these rights. Hampden's defence of his refusal to pay ship-money rested upon the absolute rights of property and the majority verdict of the judges against him turned moderate opinion against the king's personal rule as endangering the security of the subjects' rights.

The parliamentary interpretation of rights under the constitution was as one-sided as the king's, and allowed no adequate solution of the problem of government. Whitelocke had urged in parliament as early as 1610 that the power of the king in parliament was supreme over all other powers in the kingdom, including the king's independent prerogative, but this was no answer to the constitutional difficulty unless its radical implications were accepted. A sovereign power in which the king refused to co-operate and was legally entitled to do so was likely to be unworkable and to leave the government under the existing law. When the opposition accepted Whitelocke's argument in 1641 it was soon forced to deny to the king any public position at all.

The religious differences exacerbated the constitutional. James rejected puritanism on political grounds but Charles was alienated by its theological and ethical outlook. Under his patronage a minority of the clergy, led by Laud, rose to ecclesiastical power and used the royal supremacy for a genuine reformation in which Roman Catholic corruptions and Calvinist innovations were removed from the Church of England. This minority taught the divine right of episcopacy in opposition to the divine right of presbytery. It also defended the king's right to rule as divine, exalted his prerogative and stressed the duty of subjects to obey God's law without resistance to the king. Laud's social ideals as much as his religious reformation depended upon the royal prerogative supported by an independent church, clerically governed and sufficiently endowed to act as a separate estate of the realm. King and convocation were to order not only the religious life but much of the social conduct of Englishmen. He thought that the social evils of his day were to be corrected only by the prerogative enlightened by true spiritual leaders

Laud's work produced an outburst of anti-clericalism, anti-popery and hostility to prerogative government. The canons of 1640 were denounced in parliament as a usurpation of parliamentary power and it was resolved by the House of

THE CONSERVATIVE REVOLUTION

Commons that the clerical authority had no power to bind clergy or laity "without common consent of parliament". Parliament was more concerned with converting the royal into a parliamentary supremacy than in "true reformation".

Charles I's personal government turned moderate opinion against him but it proved its moderation by waiting for the occasion when the king's needs should compel him to summon parliament. Scottish resistance to religious changes in 1637, leading to an organized opposition in 1638, was too strong to be crushed by the king, and in 1640 the English parliament was summoned.

Charles pushed to extremes the work of his father's last years in Scotland and produced a national revolt against the prerogative. Deluded by James' pretentious claims "to be sovereign monarch, absolute prince, judge and governor over all persons, estates and causes, both spiritual and temporal", and believing firmly with his father "that whatsoever his majesty should determine in the external government of the church, with the advice of the archbishops, bishops and a competent number of the ministry should have the strength of a law", by virtue of the royal prerogative, Charles yielded to the advice of Laud and resolutely introduced innovations in the church which aroused the laity against his government.

James' cautious introduction of episcopacy had not destroyed the presbyterian framework but subjected the church courts to supervision and control in the interests of ecclesiastical peace and political security. James had to urge his bishops, in whom there was little of the hierarchical and sacerdotal outlook, to greater assertions of their authority. Most of them were anxious for the support of the church assemblies, many connived at dissent, and discipline was enforced with great moderation. Only deference to the king led many of the bishops to accept the Perth Articles (1618). The Confession of Faith of 1616 retained the rigid statement of the Calvinist doctrine of election and reprobation.

Charles appointed to bishoprics a number of clergy favourable to his views and willing to convert the Church of Scotland to a sacerdotal view of the ministry, episcopacy by divine right, sacramental and ritualistic worship, and the Arminian doctrine of grace. The church system fashioned by James was used to mould the thought and faith, conduct and worship, of the laity in ways alien to the people's habits and convictions. Charles made this clear when he compelled the bishops to issue the Book of Canons in 1636 and to use in public worship a new prayer book in close agreement with the English prayer book. The attempt in 1637 to use the new book led to the riots and petitions out of which came the National Covenant and war with Charles. The king had made no preparation beforehand to overcome resistance and was unable to decide on a statesmanlike policy after his will had been publicly defied.

The way in which the Book of Canons was issued by royal authority alone, imposing a liturgy as yet unpublished and demanding the recognition of the king's authority in ecclesiastical matters as the same as that of godly Jewish kings and Christian emperors, raised the issue of the king's authority in the church. James' bishops may have agreed with Archbishop Spottiswoode that "the king is Pope now, and so shall be" but their plea that the king's wishes respecting the Perth Articles were to be obeyed rested upon the argument that the Articles were indifferent, and not scripturally compulsory. Charles claimed to authorize matters of divine right: it was his duty as a Christian king to compel the church to observe and obey what was divinely ordained.

Few of the laity were able to debate these high principles: that was left to a number of able presbyterian divines. However, the laity were quick to see that the rejection of Charles' religious policy was only to be justified by appealing to a "free assembly" as a judge other than Charles and his episcopal favourites of what was divine. The religious controversy was between rival claims to divine right.

The conflict was between the laity and the king. The clergy had come to accept episcopacy and the Perth Articles. The nobles, whose alliance with the king had forced the church to accept these innovations, were estranged from Charles by his threat to revoke the grants of church lands to the nobility and by the commutation of tithes, which reduced the power of the nobles over tithe-payers. The employment of bishops in the king's government was an additional threat to the nobility.

Another grievance of the laity was the unusual weight of taxation after 1625 when Charles' wars with Spain and, later, France, strained his finances. The nobles placed themselves in 1637 at the head of a popular lay movement aroused by the king's ritualistic innovations and no doubt expected to keep control of it.

It was difficult for the laity to find constitutional grounds for resisting the king. The nobles had aided the passage of statutes exalting the prerogative. Through the Lords of the Articles, the king controlled parliament. There were few legal precedents and few parliamentary privileges to justify resistance or to bring pressure on the king. Rebellion in terms of the old feudal "bands" was discredited. The laity had to fight the king on his own ground and to deny to him the office in the church which he claimed. Such a divine claim was not to be countered by theories of parliamentary sovereignty.

The laity accepted the king's self-confessed obligation to enforce God's law in the church but denied that Charles' innovations were according to that law. It was argued that the divine law was to be defined by an organ, the General Assembly, in which the king played a minor part, and the king was bound on his own admission to accept and enforce its decisions. The king's independent prerogative need not be denied so long as the ends for which it existed were determined by another authority than the king. This theory underlies the National Covenant of 1638. Loyalty to the king and loyalty to God were reconciled in the obedience of king and subject to God's law.

God's law became for the Scots what the common law was for the English—a fundamental law determining the ends and purposes by which political authority was guided—and, like the English, the Scots learned that appeals to fundamental law were really appeals to men and to the wills of assemblies. The dispute between Charles and the Scots was about the human authority to declare and interpret divine law: it was no answer to assert that the divine law was clear on this issue, for that rested upon human agreement.

The National Covenant expressed a negative attitude—the defence of the true religion—in the traditional form of a "band".

It assumed the king's goodwill and respect for the national conviction, avoided any bold assertion of the principle of lawful resistance, and gave no indication that the prerogative was to be guided by the church. Moderates, like English constitutionalists, still believed that the king would use his prerogative spontaneously according to the national conception of the "true" religion. The problem of coercing a king who obstinately held to the dictates of his own conscience was still ignored.

The laity relied upon a "free" assembly of the church to be held in Glasgow in November 1638. It was intended to be a kind of ecclesiastical constituent body and so the bishops had to be excluded. It was equally necessary to avoid clerical representatives in sympathy with episcopacy. James had freely used the nobility to overcome clerical opposition in his nominated assemblies and in 1638 the nobles took steps to secure a lay predominance in the Glasgow Assembly. The Tables, a committee representative of the estates and the organ of opposition to the king, revived the election of ruling elders in the church courts in order to obtain the election, largely by lay votes, of Assembly representatives supporting their programme. Nothing could have been more challenging: a church assembly packed with laymen was offensive to Charles' sacerdotal doctrines. In fact, the Assembly defied the king, asserted the independence of church courts, restored presbyterian church government and abolished episcopacy.

Not only did Charles procrastinate, but also allowed the opposition to see that he intended to rely upon the constitution and especially parliament of which the bishops were an integral part, to frustrate the work of the Glasgow Assembly by upholding statutes clearly restricting ecclesiastical independence. In 1639 he prorogued parliament in which the Lords of the Articles, chosen in the absence of the bishops, were beyond his control, but in 1640, claiming to act with the king's "tacit consent . . . and presumed allowance" and not "to trench on sovereignty", parliament met and abolished episcopacy, the clerical estate in parliament and the Lords of the Articles. It passed a Triennial Act, with effective machinery to secure its meeting once in three years, delegated its power to a permanent committee when it was not in session, and ordered that the

Covenant should be signed by all subjects. There were even hints that it might be lawful to depose the king.

It was generally recognized that a revolutionary government was in power, the old constitution overthrown and the monarchy bound by new legal limitations. The Scots had acted more swiftly and drastically than the English parliament. The strength and efficiency of the government were due to the Committee of Estates and to its intimate connection with the Commission of the Church. The substitution of parliamentary for royal rule followed in time and reflected the policy of the Assembly: the constitutional changes were made in a short session of ten days in June 1640.

Charles was unable to repel an invasion of England connived at by the English opposition and was forced to summon the Long Parliament. At once he faced a challenge which dwarfed his Scottish problems and indirectly protected the work of the Scottish revolution. Indeed, in 1641, Charles had hopes of an understanding with the Scots on account of the English parliaments' indifference to a Scottish alliance. Charles attended the Scottish parliament in 1641. He was not allowed to confirm the Acts of 1640 which were held valid and had to assent to an act requiring the more important officers of state to be appointed after consulting parliament. The king had agreed to measures in Scotland which were in advance of what the English had claimed hitherto, and given legal confirmation to a constitution in which parliamentary government was secured.

Whatever chance there was of both sides co-operating under this constitution was ended by the presbyterian crusade launched by the extremists in 1643 on the assumption that Charles' victory in England must end the new constitution in Scotland. The fact that this had been won by the laity initially through a free General Assembly prevented in Scotland the final consummation of the English revolution—the parliamentary claim to be the sovereign law-making body. A free assembly meant the restoration of the presbyterian church in its own right. The danger of conflicting jurisdictions, as under Melville, did not arise because the same party controlled ecclesiastical and civil government until 1648.

The restoration of the church influenced Scottish development in a second way. Its logical and consistent principles provided the basis of a genuine alternative to the king's government and gave it an authoritative sanction. The Scottish parliament did not have to debate first principles but the methods and means to give them effect. In partnership with the church it not only enjoyed a reflected divine right and a moral claim to obedience, but also shared fundamental doctrines and a system of government too strong to be undermined by Levellers and Independents.

In England the assertion of parliamentary sovereignty meant the settling of first principles and consequently violent debate. It led to claims of popular sovereignty and to democratic and socialistic deductions of natural rights because of the individualistic freedom of interpretation of divine law. The puritans had to work through parliament instead of a free assembly. The claim of sovereignty was inferior to the claims of divine right, and parliament failed to establish a presbyterian church as co-partner in the struggle with the king and later with the sectaries.

The national agreement behind the National Covenant was paralleled in England by the national support for the early work of the Long Parliament. The eleven years of personal government by Charles united moderates and extremists in opposition to the policy and principles, agents and instruments, of prerogative government. The law was put above king and subject as the source of prerogative and liberty, as deciding their rival claims, and as holding the commonwealth in a balanced unity. The ambiguities and contradictory precedents of the old law, upon which king and parliamentarians had relied, were resolved by the insistence that the all-sufficient law was self-consistent, the only means of harmony, and able to determine the proper limit of co-operating agencies in the commonwealth. The law was not a collection of legal decisions and parliamentary statutes deciding in isolation and in a piecemeal way particular questions, and requiring the "artificial reason of the law" peculiar to trained lawyers for their reconciliation in one body of law. The parliamentarians appealed to a self-rationalizing, unifying and harmonizing law.

In the name of this law they attacked the king's prerogative, denied that it existed independently of other rights and demanded that it be regulated in accordance with these rights. By statute the prerogative courts and the levying of impositions and customs without parliamentary consent were forbidden. Other statutes provided for a meeting of parliament every three years and for the continuance of the Long Parliament until it agreed to a dissolution. The king, for political reasons, gave his consent and the supreme power of King in Parliament over all parts of the commonwealth was nearer general acceptance. The destruction of prerogative government was the permanent work of the Long Parliament because it was carried through by constitutional means.

The destruction of Strafford, Charles I's great minister during his personal government, clearly illustrates the new conception of law. Unable to prove that Strafford had acted treasonably as the law stood, the parliamentary majority accepted the view that Strafford's treason was against the "being of the law" because the unity of king and people, possible on the basis of law, was disrupted by Strafford's policy. Moderate royalists were as determined as extremists on Strafford's death and the king consented to the Act of Attainder.

It was generally agreed that the bishops shared the responsibility and odium of personal government, and even moderates criticized episcopacy by divine right, but the unity of the Long Parliament dissolved in the conflict over ecclesiastical reconstruction. The Lords were alienated by proposals of the Commons to abolish episcopacy since this invaded their own rights, especially the composition of their own House. Puritan attacks upon the familiar forms of public worship were increasingly resented. All, however, agreed that parliament was to make the religious settlement.

The religious question became a political and constitutional issue when the Irish Catholics rose in rebellion. Strong measures were necessary: an army had to be raised and taxes granted. Was the king to be trusted with such power? Did not his visit to Scotland mean that he was scheming against the English Parliament? The majority demanded that his ministers and councillors should be agreeable to parliament and trusted by it.

In the Grand Remonstrance it appealed to the country at large in defence of its demands, but the king's reckless attempt to arrest five leaders of the Commons united parliament for the last time against the king.

The legislation of 1641 had restored the balanced constitution by removing the possibility of the king governing without parliament. The king still possessed important executive powers in relation to appointments, foreign policy and defence; but he shared supreme authority with parliament, and his consent was essential. Earlier the constitution had limited the king by requiring the consent of the two houses; now it served to limit the two houses by the need of royal consent. The moderates were content to trust the king to respect the new acts to which he had given his consent and to co-operate with the two houses. The extremists insisted that the king's powers were held on trust and that he was answerable to the majority in the two houses as representative of the nation and public welfare. Neither side denied that monarchy was an integral part of the constitution, but to the extremists the king was a figurehead.

Such a radical transformation of the constitution was indefensible on other than political grounds, and the moderates had an easy task in showing that the rebellious opposition was destroying the constitution. No appeal to law could justify either the degree of control of the king which the extremists intended in order to give permanence to their work, or the ultimate power to coerce the king which their position implied. Their clearest publicists saw that the real issue was whether there existed a supreme power to make laws suitable to the political situation and to the needs of the nation. They repudiated the balanced constitution and fundamental law in favour of the final and absolute legislative sovereignty of the two houses.

Once vital divisions arose over the nature and content of fundamental law, once political needs were overriding, a final interpreter and an unquestionable maker of laws was necessary in order to justify that use of force and to restore that unity which law no longer provided. The claim of parliament to be sovereign was quickly challenged in the name of the sovereign people, but since that involved forcing Englishmen to be free and equal it failed to win general acceptance. Sovereignty exercised by a parliamentary majority or by a minority of the people was discredited by the civil wars.

The moderate royalists held to the constitution and legal rights of the king as modified by his agreement in parliament in 1641. This precedent held good after 1660 in spite of disputes about the respective powers and it was only in 1688 that the great bulk of the people acquiesced in a change of king in order to obtain royal assent to necessary amendment to the constitution. Unlike 1641 it was this general agreement which allowed constitutional changes by appeal to fundamental law and not to sovereignty. Locke, the great apologist of the Glorious Revolution, and the less important Whig pamphleteers ignored the revolutionary doctrine of sovereignty. The same general agreement permitted royalists to connive at resistance. In 1688 success sprang from the unity of the opposition; in 1642 religious fanaticism divided the opposition and ruined the constitutional compromise of 1641.

CHAPTER IV

THE RADICAL REVOLUTION

THE situation both in England and Scotland at the beginning of 1642 was unfavourable to Charles. Neither country offered him much prospect of recovering the initiative or of being able to negotiate upon equal terms. In Scotland the free General Assembly of 1638, in which the laity exercised decisive influence, had asserted its freedom from royal control and uprooted episcopacy. The king was prepared, though reluctantly, to agree that bishops were contrary to the constitution of the church of Scotland, but he was not willing to recognize that episcopacy was plainly contrary to the divine model of the church. The parliament of 1639–40 ended the royal control over the Lords of the Articles and secured its own superior authority. In 1641 parliament had forced Charles to agree to appoint such officers of state as were agreeable to it and had indeed "overturned not only the ancient State government, but fettered monarchy with chains, and set new limits and marks to the same, beyond which it was not legally to proceed".

By returning to London, Charles recognized that the new order in Scotland was too strong to be overthrown from within. The Long Parliament in England, by its attack upon the ministers and the institutions of personal government, had made certain that prerogative government should not be repeated, but it was the king's impetuous and clumsy actions which bound the strands of opposition together despite its inner contradictions and its lack of any constructive policy.

Behind the king's weakness in both kingdoms was an obvious lack of confidence in his intentions. He alienated his natural supporters and forced them to acquiesce in the bolder leadership of the more extreme opposition because of his failure to grasp how general was the indignation which his patronage of a minority had excited. By clinging to the Liturgy in Scotland, he had involved episcopacy in its rejection, and the royalists were covered with the obloquy which fell upon the bishops. The moderate episcopal party, disliking the extremes of Laud, was lost, for want of leadership, between the king and the covenanters. The same distrust of the king was evident in England. Instead of giving a frank promise to abandon the prerogative in its unpopular form and so conciliating those who still supported the legal privileges of the crown and its constitutional status, his policy lent colour to the arguments of those who suspected that the king was but manœuvring for the break-up of the opposition and a return to personal government.

As in Scotland, so in England, Charles' concern for episcopacy was unpopular. His support for the Laudian church enabled his enemies to exploit the national fear of Rome. His journey to Scotland and the rebellion of the Irish catholics in 1641 were readily misinterpreted as part of the royal strategy to overthrow the English parliament. The blame for all these rumours and suspicions was the king's, for it was ever "his constant unhappiness to give nothing in tyme; all things have been given at last; but he has ever lost the thanks, and his gifts have been counted constrained and extorted".

Grudging in his concessions, his opponents in Scotland knew not where to stay their hand lest he should be left with power sufficient to restore bishops and liturgy. Security was not assured: "so whatever the Prince grants, I feare we presse more than he can grant; and when we are fully satisfied, it is likely we will begin where we have left off". So indeed it happened until the Scots did "possess Assemblies and Parliaments according to our mind, and these are sovereigne medicines against the sudden return of such mortall diseases among us".

Distrust of Charles I had led to a curtailment of the powers of the monarchy itself. In Scotland the Earl of Montrose was anxious for a just settlement of the conflict which would protect the church as well as the crown, and the country as well as the estates, but few were ready to follow him in his confidence that Charles had learnt wisdom and was prepared to work with his subjects. Montrose had appealed to Charles I in 1641 to visit Scotland in order to satisfy his subjects already disillusioned by the failure of "a new heaven and a new earth" to appear, and therefore "desirous of a rechange to the former estate". He warned Charles not to aim at "absoluteness" but to allay the fears aroused by "superstitious worship" and by "the laws infringed and there liberties invaded".

Montrose was one of the original leaders of the Covenanters, and even when he joined the king's party he never lost his early dislike of episcopacy. He was anti-clerical and soon alienated from the Covenanters by the theocratic threat behind their policy, especially by the results of making signature of the Covenant compulsory upon all inhabitants, a demand initially supported by Montrose. He was also a constitutionalist in the sense that he believed that the powers of king, officers and subjects were prescribed by a constitution. He was alarmed by the rise of the Earl of Argyle to leadership, by hints that Argyle sought a dictatorial authority in the land North of the Forth, and by the increasing encroachments of parliament upon the king's prerogative. He called on Charles to practise "the temperate government", but also to free his subjects from their fear, in which case "firm obedience" would follow. The Scots had "no other end but to preserve their Religion in purity and their Liberties entire. That they intend the overthrow of monarchical government is a calumny. They are capable of no other for many and greater reasons".

Montrose's ideal was expressed in a letter "on the supreme Power in Government of all sorts". It is an important illustration of the way in which men were able to think of a supreme power beyond control and yet within a constitutional order. It expressed the aims of many conservatives who repudiated divine hereditary right as a revolutionary conception but accepted the prerogative as not answerable to parliament. Montrose was indebted to the lawyers rather than to the divines, and accepted limitations which were contradictions to them.

Civil society, he argued, needed government, and government was impossible without a sovereign power, able to enforce obedience for public good. This power was inalienable, indivisible and incommunicable, and no kind of mixed government was feasible. Sovereignty existed in all states whatever the form of government. There was no power above it and no means of rescinding its acts. But this power of sovereignty was not unlimited. It was limited by the laws of God and nature, and by the fundamental laws of the country "which are those upon which sovereign power itself resteth, in prejudice of which a King can do nothing; and those also which secure to the good subject his honour, his life, and the property of his goods."

The government of "free subjects" is sovereign, but not despotic. They should aim to get security of religion and just liberties, "the matter on which the exorbitancy of a prince's power doth work; which being secured, his power must needs be temperate and run in the even channel". Their liberties were contained in laws, and parliament "the bulwarks of the subjects' liberties in monarchies", was able to advise new laws against emergent occasions which prejudiced their liberties. But the people were not to limit royal power nor to determine what was the king's and what was theirs, for such a distinction required more than "human sufficiency".

Montrose saw that sovereignty was necessary in order to avoid tyranny, not of the king, injurious as that might be, but of the men of local power, and because sovereignty was the only escape from the rule of force, whether by sovereign or subjects. Montrose's sovereignty was the product and not the producer of the constitution. His parliament was the guardian of liberties but not the government. His theory was only possible when the law was accepted by all parties. In Scotland the law itself was disputed and was the issue behind the struggle for power. His resistance to an aggressive parliament was easily swept aside.

In 1642 the English royalists were provoked by the extremism of the parliamentary majority inspired by distrust of Charles. Though parliament was united for the last time by Charles' attempt to arrest Pym and his four colleagues, there was a real division between the parties over the best way to guarantee the constitution. From the beginning of 1642, Charles took as his advisers moderate royalists like Falkland and Hyde, later the Earl of Clarendon, and abandoned his exaggerated prerogative in favour of the traditional rights of the crown. It was Hyde's policy to insist that the crown was an integral part of the English constitution, and that its rights rested upon law. Parliament also had its rights but it was not to usurp an authority over the king. Hyde aimed at a mixed government of king, House of Lords and House of Commons in which their co-operation under the law secured the legitimate rights and powers of each.

In such a scheme the king was bound by law and was largely financially dependent on parliament, but exercised an independent power in matters of executive action, of foreign policy and appointments to office, and retained a veto upon parliamentary bills. The House of Commons was in a position to paralyse government but was unable to influence policy except indirectly and at the risk of political deadlock. The king, like parliament, was subject to law, but that did not mean that he was subject to parliament.

The royalists were distinguished by their steadfast adherence to the view that forcible resistance to legally constituted authority was unjustifiable, but they were not on that account apologists for absolutism. They admitted that the king was bound by any law which was the result of the joint action of the whole parliament, and also that he was to be disobeyed were he to violate that law. They admitted that the king was not absolute, but they denied that he was to be compelled to observe the limits of the law. To withhold support and to refuse co-operation were adequate means to thwart unlawful absolutism, and less dangerous to the fundamental order of society.

The weakness of the royalist position was the same as that of Montrose's ideal. Both had to assume that the king was willing to co-operate with his subjects, and, though liable to be misled by his ministers, would never deliberately pursue aims detested by the people. A king who was able to abuse his powers without being compelled to return to his constitutional limits was only a limited king in a peculiar sense, and in a sense which made it all the more important that he should observe willingly the constitution. It was unlikely to prove workable when king and parliament were bent on following different policies.

Distrust of the king stimulated a radical movement in both England and Scotland. He was to be reduced to but "the sign of a king" by being forced to agree to severe constitutional restrictions. His ministers and his policies were to be determined by his parliaments. In both countries the opposition to the king later split into moderates, willing to show trust in the king's sincerity in coming to an understanding, and the extremists, who had lost all trust in the king and required him to be their tool.

There were, however, great differences in the radicalism of the two countries. In England, presbyterianism was unable to establish itself. The sects grew rapidly in the disorder of the early years of the Civil War. The demand for toleration not only prevented the relation of church and state, which the presbyterian sought, from being established, but also contained a more fateful challenge. Parliament was largely opposed to the sectaries, and the dependence of parliament upon the people began to be urged with increasing violence. Principles formulated by a presbyterian parliament against the king were now applied by the sectaries against parliament. Radical political reforms were demanded.

Since the sectaries were most active in the army and found their protection in its power, the clash of parliament and army was to shake the foundations of the state. Republicanism and popular sovereignty were urged against king and parliament. Individualism and natural rights were used to defend the liberty and equality of all men. Secularism became more widespread; but there were also those who based political power upon the conscience. The English civil wars ended in the triumph of a sect over the nation, and in the irreconcilable opposition of the republican parliament and the army resolved to limit parliamentary sovereignty by certain unalterable constitutional guarantees.

The radical development in Scotland never lost its social discipline in sectarian liberty. Presbyterianism had become the native expression of ecclesiastical independence, and at the same time the partner of aristocratic government. It stood for the uniformity of a national church and against any toleration. The individual judgment was strictly held to the divine order, interpreted by the church as a whole. The people were not regarded as the source of ecclesiastical power and as directing their pastors according to the Word. There were no sects in Scotland until the Cromwellian occupation, when the civil power no longer lent support to the church.

The revolt in Scotland against Charles I had been both religious and political; the victorious party ruled in both church and state, and permitted neither religious nor political deviations. There were no sects, no rights of conscience, no appeal to natural rights and no declarations of popular sovereignty. There was not even an open expression of republicanism—the attachment to monarchy was too strong even for the zealots to repudiate. There was, therefore, in Scotland no hint of political radicalism no radical transformation of the state's attitude to the church, and no sign of individualistic democracy. The rule of parliament and General Assembly was secured: the Scottish army tended to be the instrument of political power and did not claim to decide policy.

There was, however, a radical party and a radical policy within the covenanters' successful opposition to the king. Its bid to apply the Covenant to the three kingdoms led to the conflict between the English sectaries and the Scottish presbyterians which ended directly in the occupation of Scotland, and indirectly in the collapse of the Protectorate. Another result was to divide the ruling class in the church and state into two parties and to stimulate their struggle for power. The fateful outcome of the civil wars was largely due to the different and hostile radical extremes which developed in the two countries.

During 1642 the English parliament confidently withstood the efforts of the king to raise forces in the country. Its terms to the king were presented in the Nineteen Propositions of June 1642 by which he was asked to appoint privy councillors and the great officers of state with parliamentary approval, to regulate his family and the church as parliament advised, and to agree that the militia should be entrusted to those in whom parliament had confidence.

These claims were not based upon any clear theory. Parliament denied that it was making new law and still clung to the old constitution. Parliament was anxious to appear as defending the constitution against royal invasion when, in fact, the king was being pressed to accept terms evidently contrary to his rights. Parliament had to claim that the two houses, without the king, were the supreme court of justice to declare what was the law of the land, and that none were to question its judgment. Parliament, as representing the kingdom which was most likely to know what was necessary for its own preservation, was the judge of what was the constitution.

Even when parliament defended taking up arms against the king, it did not assert a clear claim to sovereignty but argued that parliament and protestantism were threatened by total destruction. Unwilling to defend its claims by a revolutionary doctrine, unable to use the common law without strained interpretations, and yet forced to make these claims to secure itself against a king it deeply distrusted, parliament had to conjure up the spectre of a catholic and malignant party led by the king and conspiring against the rights of parliament and the true church.

The violence of parliament did most to raise an army for the king. Defence of the church against parliamentary zealots, who proposed to go much further than the act passed with Charles' consent to deprive bishops of temporal power and of courts of jurisdiction, began the recruitment of the king's party. Under Hyde's tuition, the king appeared as the defender of the constitution. It was only after parliament insisted in September 1642 that it should keep its forces together until the king surrendered to its jurisdiction all those voted by parliament to be delinquents, and that the cost of the parliamentary army was to be met by such delinquents and other malignant persons, that those who had been neutral and reluctant to take sides were forced to identify themselves with the king. At the close of 1642 Charles had an army which was able to secure what advantages there were from the drawn battle of Edgehill. Essex, the parliamentary commander, retreated towards London but was reinforced at Turnham Green by the train-bands of the city, and the king was forced in turn to retreat to Oxford.

In 1643 the war extended to the north and the west. In Yorkshire, the possession of Hull and of the main clothing towns gave the parliament the advantage, until the earl of Newcastle relieved York, and began an offensive which at Adwalton Moor on 30th June, 1643, was so successful as to leave parliament only the port of Hull. In the west, the parliamentary general, Waller, after some success, suffered a serious defeat at Roundway Down, on 13th July, 1643, and Bristol was forced to surrender to the royalists. The king's hopes to move the successful armies in the north and west against London in conjunction with his own army were frustrated by local interests. The king aimed, then, to capture Gloucester, the one remaining stronghold of parliament in the west, between Bristol and Lancashire. Thwarted by Essex who was greatly aided by the London train-bands, an indecisive battle was fought at Newbury in September 1643, but the king was forced to let Essex return to London.

Neither side, therefore, had the advantage and what was at first expected by parliament to be a demonstration of parliamentary strength in the country against the king was proving a protracted struggle. Pym, as the leader of the middle party in the Commons, had managed to persuade parliament to take the steps necessary to conduct the war without splitting over the ultimate aims. Armies were raised, taxes levied, and administration organized with success sufficient to enable the king not to return to London in triumph. Pym's aims were to force the king to agree to those concessions without which the early work of the Long Parliament could not be guaranteed against the king's secret hostility, especially by insisting that his ministers must have the confidence of parliament and by denying the king's right to take the advice of anyone he chose. Pym also upheld a puritan Church of England.

His was a conservative resistance, directed to hold Charles I to the law, but not to destroy monarchy and not to deny his right to the throne. None the less, Pym realized that either the king or parliament must grow less, and sought to place in parliament those powers which the king was no longer trusted to employ under the law. He wished the war to be continued until the king accepted his fate and admitted parliament as the judge and upholder of the law over the prerogative. He never seemed to doubt that the king would have to yield in the end, that the parliamentary demands were not incompatible with a legal monarchy, and that parliament was unlikely to become an arbitrary government in the very process of preventing arbitrary government by the king.

The Solemn League and Covenant was Pym's great work in the House of Commons, although it was accepted only in consequence of the defeats incurred by parliamentary armies in the north and the west. He himself urged parliament to accept the Scottish terms for the ratification of the Solemn League on the grounds that the greater danger was from the king and that the abolition of episcopacy was no onerous payment to make in order to avert the collapse of the parliamentary cause.

The agreement between the English parliament and the Scots was negotiated and ratified in very different spirits in Edinburgh and London. The English wanted a civil alliance: the Scots insisted on religious uniformity, and believed that both peoples had entered into a most solemn covenant before God, binding unto eternity, whatever a future parliament might do. For the Scots, the Solemn League and Covenant rested upon the divine right of presbytery. In the English parliament there were few supporters of Scottish presbyterianism, although it had many champions among the ministers of the city of London, whose influence on parliament was noteworthy.

By the Solemn League and Covenant, sworn on 13th October, 1643, the two parliaments undertook "the preservation of the true Protestant reformed religion in the church of Scotland in doctrine, worship, discipline and government, and the reformation of religion in the Church of England according to the Word of God and the example of the best reformed Churches", and extended it to Ireland also. This last innovation was introduced by the Westminster Assembly, a conference of divines summoned by parliament to give advice on the reformation of the Church of England, and approved by the English parliament. In accordance with this purpose, the Scots sent an army into England under Leslie, now Earl of Leven, in January 1644, and it soon began to influence the course of the struggle.

From the outset of the Civil War in England, the extremists among the Scots had openly sympathized with the English parliament, had pressed the king to come to an understanding with it, and hoped for a uniformity of religion in both countries. The General Assembly of July 1642 welcomed an approach from the English parliament and urged on it the presbyterian reformation. Representations were made to the Scottish privy council, and the Assembly set up a standing committee of its leading members to press its case. The privy council was too overawed by the demonstrations of gentry and burgesses to give any support to the king's proposal that it should mediate.

The king could not even rely upon the neutrality of the Covenanters. When the English parliament appealed for help after the battle of Edgehill, Charles sent a vindication of his actions. The privy council decided by a small majority to publish it, and not the parliament's appeal, but under renewed pressure of gentry and ministers the council agreed to the publication of that appeal. A counter or Cross Petition by the royalists urged the council to respect the due rights of the king and not to disturb the peace of the church or country. At once the Assembly's Commission issued warnings to be read from every pulpit and ordered every presbytery to act against any who sought signatures to the royalist petition.

A Convention of Estates met on 22nd June, 1643, declared itself a fully competent body and set aside the limitations which the king prescribed. With the Convention working intimately with the General Assembly, which met on 2nd August, so that the nobles attended the Assembly in the morning and the Convention in the afternoon, the Covenanters were in control of the country, and, though inclined at first to a kind of armed mediation until its impracticability was made clear, their policy was to unite with the English parliament against the king. These movements were hastened by the revelation of Charles' agreement with the Irish rebels for a cessation or truce for twelve months, from which in fact he obtained little help and much discredit.

The Solemn League and Covenant of 1643 was much more a party measure than the National Covenant of 1638, and even the friends of the party were critical. Under the orders of the Convention of Estates and by the efforts of the Assembly's Commission, the new covenant was to be sworn by men and women, and subscribed by the men of each congregation, under penalty of excommunication and confiscation of goods. It was important as recognizing the common cause with the English parliament against the king, but it was much more significant as a party programme requiring the creation and triumph of similar parties in the two other kingdoms, and compelling the king to accept the party line.

The attitude of the Covenanters is to be seen in the extreme claims of Johnston of Wariston, the most fearless and consistent of their leaders. To him episcopal government was contrary to God's will, so that he condemned the defection of the Scottish church "first in longing with the Jews to be ruled as the other nations about us, wearying of God's spiritual governement, casting of his yok, and saying that we wold not suffer him to rule over us, who had his kingly office honorabler erected, spiritualer established, and longer practised heir. . . ." It was natural for him to describe the liturgy introduced into Scotland by Charles I as, "brought in to droune us in superstition," and, by reason of the revolt against it, as "God's dischclout to scoure the vessels of his sanctuarie from the filthiness of the ceremonies". When urged to be moderate in his advice to the aristocratic leaders of the revolt, he declared ". . . his mynde of not bounding, minching, carving be halfes as God's cause". Proudly he pointed to "the paralel betwixt Israel and this churche, the only tuo sworne nations to the Lord" and studied God's dealing with the Jews and "their voyage . . . that we may learne to marke his dealing with our auin Izrael". Here was the justification of the covenants, which "keeped the Lord as it wer in a legal possession of his right and priviledges, whereof he was violently robbed by men's tyrannie . . .".

Robert Baillie was a less rigid covenanter than Wariston but he made it clear what the covenants meant to the Scots. He was one of the Scottish Commissioners who attended the Westminster Assembly, and he joined in the vigorous defence of the presbytery which the commissioners had undertaken. To the English it was a "strange monster", though no people were more in need of presbytery owing to their being "inclinable to singularities, to differ from all". It would have been "an impossibility ever to have gotten England reformed by humane means, as things here stood, without their brethrens help. The learnedest and most considerable part of them were fullie Episcopall; of those who joyned with the Parliament, the greatest and most countenanced part were much Episcopall".

It was against this background that Baillie stated that the National Covenant was against all episcopacy and the Solemn League and Covenant was for the rooting out of "a meer humane invention, without the word of God". It was essential to covenanting theory to show that ruling elders (the laity chosen to sit in the church courts) were by divine right, for "we admit of no officers in the house of God, on ane humane and ecclesiastick right". Therefore, the elders were not the deputies of the people, but the officers of God. The general covenanting view was that the whole congregation, or each church, had no divine right "to give voice and suffrage in matters of government"; nor indeed had the kirk-session, for it was the presbytery which was to ordain and excommunicate. To some, indeed, the kirk-session was but a commission with delegate power from the presbytery.

The importance of the divine right of presbytery was shown by the letter of the Assembly of 1642 to the English parliament urging uniformity in religion and arguing that "the Prelatical Hierarchy being put out of the way, the work will be easy without forcing of any conscience", since presbyterianism was "*jure divino* and perpetual", whereas "almost universally" no such claim was made for Episcopacy. The point was made even more vividly by Samuel Rutherford against the critics of presbyterianism when he defiantly retorted that the General Assembly might not "force the conscience of the poorest beggar".

Arbitrary government in matters left to human choice was a tyranny over conscience. The church had but a "ministerial" power to declare what was, and what was contrary to, the law of God. The law of God, God's will, was sovereign. The church had no power to free any one from God's law and consequently no power to tolerate. The conscience was bound by and to God's law, and not what the individual conscience thought that law to be. Obviously, the earthly interpreter of the law was all-important and to presbyterianism it was the Assembly: and yet Rutherford affirmed that no Assembly was infallible.

The Scots assumed that the English parliament was pledged to these principles, and their army contributed greatly to freeing the North of England from royalist influence. At

Marston Moor, 2nd July 1644, the king's army was decisively defeated by the parliamentary armies and the Scots, who then turned back to besiege Newcastle. Leven was also hampered by the anxiety aroused in Scotland by Montrose's spectacular campaigns in the year following his return in August 1644. In his six victories, Montrose had crushed the Covenanting armies in Scotland, but in September 1645 he was completely routed at Philiphaugh by a force detached from the Scots army in England.

Leven's limited activity in the North was regretted by the English presbyterians and the Scottish Commissioners in London, who grasped that there would be no true reformation until the Scots army gave hope of persuading the divided English to honour the covenant. Meanwhile, a great step had been taken by the English parliament in the creation of the New Model Army under Sir Thomas Fairfax and Oliver Cromwell. Paid by parliament, the cavalry being mainly veterans of the Eastern Association and enthusiasts for the cause, and the pressed recruits and survivors of earlier campaigns, who constituted the infantry, being subjected to a strict discipline, this army at last offered the means of a rapid conclusion to the civil war.

The decisive battle was fought at Naseby on 14th June, 1645. The next months were occupied with sieges, and in May 1646 Charles joined the Scots army before Newark in the hope that it would help him against the English, but he found himself in fact its prisoner. The aim of his last years was to exploit the differences between his enemies, and to make full use of what he thought was his remaining weapon—that his enemies could not do without him.

To the Scots the position was simple. "The Covenant now will doe all his business," and nothing less would protect him. "He must either yield to reason, and altogether change his principles, or else he will fall in tragick miseries." The king's obstinacy was infuriating. "If we desyre to deall truelie with the heart of a man obstinate near to induration, we would use some probable means of persuasion." But in fact they had no means of persuasion, and "if the King will not return on just termes, what to do with him we cannot tell". They were resolved "not to divide from England on any termes". Therefore the Scots came to an agreement with the English parliament, receiving half of the expenses due to them, evacuating their army and leaving the king in England since they were unwilling to risk a break with England unless Charles accepted their terms. To preserve the Covenant as the fundamental law of Scotland, the presbyterians were forced to abandon the king.

It was equally evident that they had failed to secure the covenant in England. The English parliament was too conscious of its sovereignty to accept the limitations underlying the Covenant. First, it resolved to settle religion in England with the advice of the Westminster Assembly, but that Assembly was limited by the instructions of parliament. Baillie described two-thirds of parliament as being composed of some Independents, "small but prime"; lawyers, to whom church government was a civil affair, (parliament constituting the church); and worldly, prophane men who feared the ecclesiastical yoke. Never were pope and king more earnest for the headship of the church than "the plurality of this parliament". Parliament, as much as the army, was against the Westminster Assembly, the City of London and the body of ministers. It set up in 1645-6 "but a lame Erastian Presbytery", limiting discipline to certain categories, allowing civil supervision and providing for two ruling elders to every minister in the church assemblies.

Secondly, parliament seemed to Baillie to be against "any shadow of a king", though it might permit Charles to be "a Duke of Venice". The Scots could not assent to the parliament's claim to settle religion and control the militia without granting any share to the king; and yet they expected Charles to take the covenant and to follow the advice of his parliaments "hard pills to be swallowed by ane willful and unadvysed Prince". Wariston, who had earlier studied the Calvinist defenders of limited monarchy and of armed defence against absolutist rulers, and in reading a puritan treatise on the superiority of the church to its governors had left "blanks for a civil paralel", pleaded as much as "all the royalists in Scotland" for "the crowne and the King's just power" against the English parliament. Some years later he was to repent of his defence of the rights of the crown. Even Rutherford, more inclined to republicanism than the other covenanting leaders, was not against monarchy provided that it was "lawful and limited", although he preferred a mixed government in which the king had a fiduciary power on behalf of the people.

The Covenanters held to the idea of the covenanted king. The Covenant was a joint declaration of king and people that the law of God should be a fundamental law. The king's power and that of parliament were determined and defined by that law, and to be obeyed only as its instruments. There was no clash of jurisdictions and no claim to absolute power. Observance of God's law reconciled the differing claims to loyalty. The General Assembly, free and independent by divine right, was the interpreter of God's law but did not claim a power to impose it on the people. In the Scottish parliaments and assemblies from 1640–8, the same party was in power and was able to achieve the closest co-operation. In the politics of those years the idea of the covenanted king meant that the king was to work with this party.

The rise of the Independents and their relation to the Separatists were noted in 1641, and within a very few years their radical doctrines and the still more extreme ones associated with the many sects which were fostered by Independency were exercising a powerful influence. The Independents were a middle group between the presbyterians and the sects. They used against the presbyterians their own arguments, just as in turn the sects developed the Independents' arguments according to their own experience.

The Independents were opposed to the presbyterian national church and covenanted uniformity. Conscious of being a minority, their plea was for latitude and toleration. The fear of presbyterianism led the Independents to modify the presbyterian attitude to the civil power. As the critics of presbyterianism and of parliament, when it tended to a spiritual "tyranny", and as the advocates of toleration, the Independents gained the support of the extremer sects, until these applied Independent principles to new issues of political representation and property, when it was the turn of the Independents to reject such extreme allies.

The presbyterians had argued against the tyranny of episcopacy on the ground that the enforced conformity to such human inventions on prudential grounds violated the conscience which was under the government of the spirit. They had pleaded that in matters left indifferent by the Scriptures it was slavery to subject men to worldly authority. They held that force was no way of convincing the conscience and therefore the state was to deal with the body and external activities, and not to usurp spiritual power. Thus, the human discipline of the episcopal order was set aside.

The presbyterian system was just as human to the Independents. They found no Scriptural warrant for a national scheme of presbyteries and synods and Assembly in which the majority prevailed; no justification for binding an individual church of those held together by similar conscientious convictions to the judgment of the delegates of other churches. They admitted willingly enough a right of brotherly criticism and censure, but not a jurisdiction. They rejected an alien, external and imposed authority: "the meanest man's reason, specially in matters of faith and obedience to God, is to be preferred before all authority of all men".

An Assembly to interpret the Scriptures by authority would be to eke out light in divine things by human prudence. The Independents looked forward to further illumination—to the law in the heart than to the divine prescription of the presbyterians. The Scriptures had to be applied to new and to particular conditions, and reason was the means, even for presbyterians, but the Independents tended to unite reason and conscience. To the presbyterians, toleration meant setting up human ideas against the divine truth: to the Independents, presbyterian uniformity denied God's power in the conscience by substituting a human authority dependent on the state. To the presbyterians, the Old Testament offered a model: to the Independents, the Gospel freed men from the Law of Moses and from human ordinances.

The Independents were very tolerant of the more extreme views which grew up within their churches. In the same way, their stress on toleration, on the freedom of the conscience and of the right reason of the Elect, underlay their church government. As the Gospel had to be freely accepted, so also had the decisions of a church to be the decisions of the members.

Authority was not enough, not even that of the majority, and certainly not that of the organs of the church. Collective authority sprang from the conviction of the conscience and reason of each, especially in all disciplinary matters. "In the cognition of these causes, every member of the Congregation must be satisfied in his mind concerning every passage of every action; for they doe not proceed by the plurality of numbered voyces, but with the harmonious consent of all who have right to voyce."

This attempt to incorporate the conscience of each in the judgment of the whole was possible only when none was compelled to be a member, that is, when those who shared convictions were free to separate from those who were indifferent. So necessary was this community of conviction that obstinate dissenters within the congregation had to be purged from it in order to avoid rule by majorities. If "any doe dissent from the most, they appoint in that case paines to be taken for the information of the dissenters that they may consent; but if these paines prove fruitlesse and the Dissenters refuse to joyn with their brethren, they are declared obstinate, and to have lost the right of voycing for that time. Yea ... they appoint all who continue in their dissent in any matter of weight, to be farther proceeded with for their contumacy". For the same reasons, they made trial of the "sociable and complying disposition of the person to be admitted, with the spirits of the whole Church whereof he is to be a member".

A Covenanter like Rutherford had insisted that rulers had to respect man as "*res sacra*" and not "make merchandise of the living temples of the Holy Ghost". The Independents concluded that the individual's integrity required his active participation in government and the dependence of rulers upon the people as the "first original and Maker, the free will of the promiscuous multitude". They claimed that matters of opinion and of outward form in religion were to be ruled by every man's conscience, light and reason, and that rulers and parliaments were to be forbidden to interfere. Some were supposed to allow every man to decide whether to obey civil laws in matters indifferent. The expediency and reason of such laws must convince the subject's conscience.

Such was the harvest of the presbyterians' appeal to the conscience in matters not prescribed clearly in the Scriptures. Still more extreme was the deduction from the presbyterians' doctrine of the Scriptures as a fundamental law. "In a free State no Magistrate hath power over the Bodies, Goods, Lands, Liberties of a free people, but by their free consent; and because free men are not free Lords of their owne estates, but are only stewards under God; therefore they may not give their free consent to any Magistrate to dispose upon their Bonds, Lands and Liberties at large as themselves please, but as God the Soveraigne Lord of all pleases; and because the Word is a perfect rule ... it will be therefore necessary that neither the people give consent nor that the Magistrate take power, but according to the lawes of the Word".

The sovereign people possessed divine rights by a divine constitution, and government existed to protect and realize such rights. The more secular idea of natural rights by the law of nature is evidently not far distant, and was introduced by the claim of the sectaries, not to a "miserable and despicable" toleration, but to a "free and absolute liberty" in all things of the mind and in matters of opinion "as the due and naturall right of every humane creature in all places of the whole earth".

The presbyterians tended to be static, but the Independents were forward-looking and this linked them to the sects. They appealed to God's purpose for the Saints, and the Millenarians applied it. In the same way the Levellers used the Independents' appeal to the sovereign people. Both were developments of the same stock. The Millenarians were inspired by the vision of Christ's kingdom on earth and of the part played by the Elect. The Levellers sharply opposed conscience to reason, the law of the spirit to the law of nature, and spiritual to secular society. To them the law of nature was God's law as the expression of reason given to all men. Equality and liberty were the ideal in secular society as in the church. Nor were they merely pious aspirations. Reason in the hands of the Levellers was a sword to cut the bonds which kept men from their birthright and to end oppression. Men were freed because their reason was freed from custom and traditions, from authority and conquest. Magna Carta was a "beggarly thing" containing many marks of intolerable bondage.

Fundamental law was not the common law, known only to lawyers, but free or right reason and common equity. "We are the men of the present age and ought to be absolutely free from all kinds of exorbitances, molestations or arbitrary power" based upon the past. Accordingly, they appealed to inalienable and natural rights, to consent, and to its regular operation through universal suffrage and frequent parliaments. It was inevitable that the Levellers appealed from parliament to people: "most Parliament men are to learn what is the just power of a parliament, what the parliament may do and what the parliament itself may not do."

No bishop, no king was now paralleled by no presbytery, no aristocracy: "without a powerful compulsive Presbytery in the Church, a compulsive Mastership or Aristocraticall government over the people in the state could never long be maintained". So "the Imperiall and absolute Soveraignty must be put in the hands of the multitude of the basest people", and the will of the multitude becomes law.

By contrast, the Millenarians were unable to trust any but the elect to carry forward God's purpose. The great work of reformation brought about during the civil war was to be safeguarded as a divine trust. The people were unfitted to determine their own good. It was not will, but insight into the divine purpose, which justified government. The Millenarians rejected the secular and democratic arguments of the Levellers and claimed the freedom of the true believers to govern for the good of the people. They petitioned against the Levellers' natural rights and law in favour of government by good men. The rule of the godly, or of the Saints, was a radical but not a politically democratic ideal. The basic conflict of these two movements helps to explain the failure of the constructive policy of the puritan revolution.

The withdrawal of the Scots left the English parliament to deal with the army. The London merchants were pressing for its disbandment. Parliament hoped to enlist many of the New Model army for service in Ireland under officers pledged to the Covenant, but its failure to deal honestly with arrears of pay drove the discontented soldiers into collaboration with those who were hostile to parliament on religious and political grounds.

Parliament relied upon London to meet the stand of the army under its democratic organization of agents or Agitators. It tried to come to terms with Charles on the moderate terms of a presbyterian establishment for three years and parliamentary control of the militia for ten years. The army seized the king, and publicly declared that it was no "mere mercinary army, hired to serve any arbitrary power of a state" but was the champion of the "people's just rights and liberties". The presbyterian leaders were forced from parliament and when the London mob attempted to influence parliament, the army marched on London.

The army leaders, Cromwell and Ireton, presented to Charles the Heads of the Proposals, which were less exacting in religion than the presbyterian terms. The king's intrigues and delays led the extremists of the army to turn from their own leaders, to appoint new Agitators and to formulate the radical constitutional claims of the Agreement of the People. Biennial parliaments chosen by manhood suffrage and sovereign save as limited by certain inalienable "native rights", were to give reality to the people's authority and government by individual consent. The debates of the Council of the Army at Putney showed the difference between the leaders and the agitators. Ireton stressed the relation of property and political rights, and the advantages of security under law. He stood for the observance of contracts, for legal rights in a traditional sense and for the people as those with a "permanent fixed interest in the kingdom". He rejected the natural rights to which the Agitators appealed, as leading to the destruction of property. Cromwell at last asserted his authority and restored the discipline of the army.

The Scots Commissioners, shocked by the army's extremism, agreed in December 1647 to the Engagement with the king, who had fled to Carisbrooke Castle. He promised to confirm the covenant in both countries by acts of parliament, to suppress heresy and to establish presbyterianism for three years. He was promised a Scots army to vindicate his just rights over the militia, to make appointments and to negative bills.

Parliament suspected such an understanding, agreed to no further addresses to the king and ended the Committee of Both Kingdoms.

The Engagement represented a reaction to the policy of the extreme party in Scotland, and throughout the early months of 1648 it steadily lost ground to the more moderate party in favour of restoring the king. The Commission of the Church drew up a declaration that the king's concessions were inadequate, but a majority of the lay members resisted the declaration. In the parliament of March 1648 the revulsion of opinion to the king's cause was most noteworthy among the representatives of the shires and burghs, who had been more sincere supporters of the covenant than the nobles.

Parliament was anxious to restore the king before making greater demands upon him; the church wanted to exact the strictest terms before giving help. Parliament proceeded to demand that monarchy and presbyterianism be restored in England and that the sectarian army be disbanded. The church set itself to hinder the raising of an army. Many of the officers of that part of the old covenanting army still under arms refused to join the new enterprise. Parliament demanded a subscription by all subjects to a declaration of willingness to defend the lawfulness of parliament and its laws, and passed an act to protect those ministers who supported the Engagement.

The extreme party, in spite of all the efforts of the church, was not able to prevent the march into England by a Scots army under the Duke of Hamilton on 8th July, 1648. Its ill-planned and mis-led adventure came to an end when Cromwell surprised it at Preston in August. It was the last effort of the moderate constitutionalists before the Restoration to break the impasse between the king and the extremists, and to save the constitution as well as to secure presbyterianism. It depended on an alliance of moderates behind the crown and of a moderate policy on the part of the crown.

Such moderation meant compromise, and the extremists were unable to yield where divine right was at stake. To them the only policy was to uphold the Solemn League and Covenant of 1643, if necessary against the king, against the English and against the moderate Scots. They were willing to fight the

English but only for the compulsory covenant and only if the army was not corrupted by co-operation with malignants. They distrusted the king and the party of Engagers. There was to be no constitutional settlement unless Charles became a truly covenanted king—that is, unless as a constitutional king of Scotland he proved himself a "constitutional" king of England by forcing presbyterianism upon it. The extreme party in Scotland was content to see the triumph of the extreme party in England. More than that: it was willing to rise to power in Scotland by a temporary alliance with the English Independents.

The royalist risings in England in conjunction with the Engagers failed to attract much support, partly because the Scots were regarded doubtfully, partly because royalists and presbyterians were unfriendly allies, and partly because the mass of the people was indifferent. The army was able to master a dangerous challenge. The renewal of the civil war had a drastic effect in increasing the influence of extremists in the army, in reducing the chance of a constitutional settlement, and in causing a minority, and military, rule.

The continued negotiations of the presbyterian parliament with Charles alienated the army, to which the king's intrigues were the main cause of war, led to the exclusion of all but fifty or sixty members by Colonel Pride from parliament, and to the setting up of a court to try the king for erecting an unlimited power in place of the limited power entrusted to him by the people. The execution of the king on 30th January, 1649, on the one hand, ended the sham of constitutional government, the attempts, now impossible, at mixed government with a king so resolute as Charles I, and the dilemma of upholding his due prerogative and the true religion at the same time. On the other hand, it opened up problems of republican government by an unrepresentative, unpopular, and unconstitutional House of Commons lacking real power of its own.

The commonwealth had to secure itself by the conquest of Ireland and Scotland. During 1649, Cromwell struck harshly at the Irish Catholics who since 1641 had expectations from the king, but had fallen into grave divisions. The invasion of Scotland took place in the summer of 1650 and at Dunbar on 3rd September Cromwell was fortunate enough to destroy the

Covenanters' army and to overthrow the rule of the extremists in the state.

The period between the battles of Preston, August 1648, and Dunbar, September 1650, was the climax of the Covenanting movement. The danger of a clash between the parliament and assembly, of state and church, and of constitutionalists and covenanters was ended by the defeat of the moderates at Preston. Once again one party ruled in church and state, bringing both into harmony. The "mystery of our weakness" was noted by one of the party in connection with the success of the Engagers in raising an army against the expressed will of the church, but news of Preston gave the party the illusion of power. A rising in the west led to the occupation of Edinburgh by the extremists under the Marquis of Argyle. The Engagers were forced to agree to submit to the church, to await the decision of parliament and assembly, and not to exercise their public offices until then. Behind this settlement was the power of Cromwell, who led his army into Scotland, was welcomed in Edinburgh and gained the assurance that the Engagers would be excluded from all public life. He left a detachment of troops to protect the new government until it had organized its own defence.

During January and February 1649 the Covenanters' policy was decided. Parliament, from which all opponents of the extreme party were excluded, passed the Act of Classes by which any who belonged to any of the four classes of opponents were to be expelled from office or public trust. All Engagers and their sympathizers, including any who had not protested against the Engagement, were affected, but also all whose life and conduct fell below the standards of the extremists. The church party thus controlled the whole range of offices and appointments. The leading Engagers were excluded for life, and the lesser offenders were only to be reappointed, after their term of exclusion, provided that the church was satisfied with their repentance. Six months later the church was to purge itself of all who had failed to further the extremists' cause.

In January, too, the Commissioners of the Church denounced the toleration and activities of the English sectaries. On February 5th, parliament declared Charles II to be King of Great Britain, France and Ireland, but on February 7th resolved that he should not exercise his power until he had sworn the Covenants and to plant presbytery in all his possessions. Thus, the attachment to monarchy was to be used to reduce the three kingdoms to the power of the extremists. Their policy lacked the odium while having the advantages of republicanism. They were playing for the highest of stakes: to beat the sectaries by supporting the king, to beat the constitutionalists by using the king against them. The prize was universal presbytery, and parliaments and king as the instruments of a party.

Behind the stress on parliaments and limited monarchy, was the unshaken belief in the divine rights of presbytery and the obligation of those who believed in this to rule. The events of 1648 had clearly proved that a parliamentary majority was not the basis of such a government. A modern historian has defended the policy of the church in that year on the ground that the parliamentary majority acted contrary to the national majority, but that was not the justification of the church party. It simply argued that the rulers were bound by and had to accept the fundamental law of the land, itself defined in agreement with the law of God, and nationally sanctioned by the Covenants. The assembly was the interpreter of the law and the "people" were those who accepted its decision.

Success rested on the acquiescence of Charles II and the defeat of Cromwell, the champion of the Commonwealth against the Scottish challenge. Charles, compelled by failure in Ireland, agreed to the Scottish terms, signed the treaty on 11th June, 1650, at sea, and took the oath to maintain the Covenants and establish presbytery, on arriving at the mouth of the Spey twelve days later. Fear of the national enthusiasm for the king, and fear of his dissembled attitude to the Covenant, led the extremists to tighten their hold on king, country and army. The Commissioners of the Church solemnly declared that "they will not own Him nor His interest otherwise than with a subordination to God and so far as He owns and prosecutes the Cause of God". The army was systematically purged of royalist supporters.

At that very time Cromwell was wasting his resources before

David Leslie's army defending Edinburgh. Forced to withdraw to Dunbar and apparently at the mercy of the Scots, Cromwell seized his opportunities on September 3rd to gain an overwhelming victory. The reign of the Scottish Saints was over; the Covenants were a bankrupt policy. Cromwell had destroyed the divine right of presbytery just as earlier he had destroyed the divine right of kings.

The extremists split into two parts after Dunbar. The one, drawing its support from the south-west, concluded that defeat could only be turned into victory by a most ruthless purge to free the rule of the elect from those corrupting elements which had called down God's anger. It had its own separate army, and in its name a Remonstrance was sent to the Committee of Estates, blaming the defeat on the unregenerate king, refusing to support his interest and demanding that all who had shown willingness to co-operate with Malignants and Engagers should be deprived of office and influence.

The Remonstrants lost their army by an unwise clash with an English force, and it became obvious, even to the majority of the church, that the Act of Classes would have to be repealed if the country was to be saved from occupation. That repeal was allowed when the Commissioners of the Church had obtained an act guaranteeing to perpetuity former acts of parliament in favour of the presbyterian religion. These supporters of the resolutions in favour of the royalists and engagers were known as Resolutioners: their opponents as Remonstrants and, later, as Protesters, who formed an irreconcilable element until the end of the century. They had no share in the campaign which ended at Worcester on 3rd September, 1651, when Charles had to abandon his realms and Scotland had to submit to occupation until 1660.

The problems raised by the schism of these "fifth-monarchy presbyterians" had been implicit in the Scottish Reformation, and throughout the controversy about presbytery. The Remonstrants declared that the majority demanded "a tyrannical and popish, and an absolute and illimitat obedience" to presbyteries even when they command "not in the Lord but contrary to the law". They refused obedience until synods and presbyteries were purged of their corrupt members.

To the Resolutioners to grant this was to abolish the foundation of presbyterian government: "for grant what subordination they pleased to a presbyterie in generall or to a presbyterie in Utopia, or any where else, yet denying it to the Presbyteries of Scotland, as now they stand" the way was open to Independency. It seemed "to overturne not only the presbyterie among us, but all government, civill and ecclesiastick in all places for ever, and brings in every where a necessitie of anarchie and confusion; that every particular person may and must follow the judgment of his own braine. . . . This extravagancie cuts the sinews of all government ever was, is or can be imagined; it makes every erroneous person the supreme judge on earth to himself of all questions, without any subjection to any power."

Thus thinking, the Resolutioners eventually came nearer to the point of view of a presbyterian minister, silenced first for opposing bishops, and later for opposing the General Assembly. "As bishops were a government but human, so is Presbyterial Government; although I confess it comes nearest to the Word of God. . . ." A colleague of his had stated in 1648 that the king should be restored unconditionally, and not to be resisted until he abused his power again, in which case it was only the abuse of his power which was to be resisted. It was on these lines that it became possible at a later date to reconcile political and religious claims.

After September 1651 the army of sectaries was triumphant. The question for the next eight years was whether the military power was capable of a constructive policy to restore civil government and reconcile the defeated interests to it. Was it possible to produce a settlement in which the individualistic, democratic aims of army circles were adjusted to the interests of landowners and merchants, in which parliamentary sovereignty and fundamental rights did not conflict, and in which puritan enthusiasm was free but without power to establish a social tyranny? As it had proved impossible in England to stabilize the work of resistance, so after 1651 it was impossible to stem the movement of reconstruction which brought about the Restoration.

The root issue behind the controversies of these years was

still being debated on the verge of the Restoration: whether *"melior an major pars"* should govern? Neither side dared to abandon its claim. To recognize the majority was to overthrow the puritan cause; to insist on the "better sort" was to lose any constitutional claim to power. There was no agreement between the army and parliament on which was the better sort.

The army never recognized the force of the parliament's claim to be its friend. Each was determined to preserve the cause for which the civil wars had been fought. To parliament, it was the sovereignty of the people's representatives, without any negative of King or Lords, and a power to make laws without any restriction. To the army the civil war had given freedom to live according to conscience as an absolute right which ought never to be at the mercy of parliamentary sovereignty, and therefore established such a negative as parliament repudiated. Moreover, the army itself was divided. It was, however, united in its opposition to monarchy. Finally, there were those, lawyers above all, who came to fear "a Fifth Monarchy" more than a *de facto* monarchy, and who preferred a monarchy with laws to the rule of the Saints, which was but a device to act arbitrarily and on grounds of necessity. On the eve of the Restoration, Wariston noted in his clear way "that the bottom of the Question is Whether the military or civil power shal be supreme or subordinate, and whether the sprite of the nation or some select party shal haive the power".

Cromwell was the undisputed leader of the army, but although he was feeling his way to some form of stable government he never succeeded in reconciling the divergent interests behind the revolution nor the defeated forces opposed to it. He was unwilling to abandon the leadership of the army for that of any other group. He was tied to its interests and ideals, even when he recognized their impracticability. His policy was to find a balance between incompatible forces, and it was his bitterest complaint that no group saw any interest other than its own, and that none would forget its quarrel. Thus, his balance was never genuine and never successful; such as it was, it was the result of his own power and directed by his sense of necessity. To Ludlow, a firm champion of parliament, Cromwell could declare: "Even if Nero were in power, it would be your duty to submit." He believed that what was good for the people, and not what pleased it, was what really mattered. The balance, which was the people's good, did not have to rest on consent.

The remnant of the Long Parliament, the Rump, a mere tenth usually, was roughly driven from its chamber on 20th April, 1653, by Cromwell just as later in the year Lilburne's soldiers drove the General Assembly from its place of meeting. The Rump had lost support, proved ineffective in its leadership, alienated the army and sought to perpetuate itself. Cromwell's action made enemies of the civilian republicans. The attempt to obtain a parliament akin to the army was discredited by the ineffectiveness of Barebone's parliament.

The army then tried a mixed government of protector, council and parliament in the Instrument of Government, which laid down that parliament was to meet for at least a period of five months in three years, and the protector's responsibility for the executive was to be limited only by parliament's partial control of taxation. Elected on a high property qualification, the new parliament refused to be a "meer eleemosynary Parliament", discussed the constitution imposed on the country, and in spite of its acceptance of the fundamentals on which Cromwell insisted, continued to object to the protector's powers. It was dissolved because of a clash over the size of the militia.

Following a cavalier rising in 1655, Cromwell attempted to rule England and Wales by eleven major-generals. It was more than military government: it was Cromwell's most determined experiment in army politics. For a year England became familiar with puritan ideals and came to hate the army and its ways. In the parliament of 1656, many republicans opposed to the protectorate were elected as a protest, and about a hundred were not allowed to take their seats. Once again the army and the republicans were bitterly hostile to each other.

To prevent military rule in the future and to restrict the executive by known law, with its right bounded as any acre of land, parliament presented the Humble Petition and Advice, in which the crown was offered to Cromwell. He refused it because acceptance would have severed him from the cause which he had led so long. The next parliament, of two houses under the new constitution, saw the return of the republicans and, after fruitless debates, a forced dissolution. Feeling was so strong in this parliament that "the House jeered when a man cited a Scripture".

The death of Cromwell on 3rd September, 1658 removed the only person able to control the army, and its quarrels with the parliamentary republicans demonstrated that neither party had learnt anything. Cromwell's compromise was also unsatisfactory. Monk, the commander in Scotland, who had purged his army of all political elements, and firmly believed that the military power was to be subordinate to parliament, marched south in January, 1660, in defence of civil authority. He learnt that the country wanted a lawful and regular parliament, and he found in the clash of the City of London and the Rump that it had lost any claim to represent the country.

Accordingly, Monk decided to allow the presbyterian members of parliament to take their seats on their agreement to provide for a new parliament, the elections to which clearly showed that the presbyterians did not enjoy public confidence. Monk permitted royalists to return to both Houses. Meanwhile, Charles II had issued the Declaration of Breda, in which his promises to his subjects were made conditional upon the wish of his parliaments. It was due to Monk that Charles' restoration was not upon explicit terms. His actions during these exciting months had been in close step with public opinion, and probably he realized that a presbyterian settlement could have had no legal force upon the king if it was rejected by the people.

If the English parliament had played some part in the Restoration and vindicated its ancient position, Scotland had no share in restoring the king. It was freed from a hateful military government. It was proud to regain its national independence. It disliked the union of the two countries imposed by the Instrument of Government, partly because of the heavy taxation, harmful to trade and alienating the towns, originally inclined to support the invaders. Its nobility was greatly impoverished. Efficient and incorrupt government, though reluctantly respected, was no substitute for parliament and assembly, suppressed in order to prevent centres of national feeling. Toleration was feared. The church, though divided, agreed that "it is to us the foundation of government that our Christian Magistrates should be thoroughly for God." Although the lesser church courts were allowed to function, their judgments were no longer enforced by the civil power. But the unfortunate consequence of Scotland having no share in the Restoration was the inability of the moderate presbyterians to exercise a decisive influence. This was all the more serious because a debating parliament as well as the assembly was associated with rebellion.

CHAPTER V

THE BLOODLESS REVOLUTION

THE years between the triumphal return of Charles II in 1660 and the ignominious flight of James II in 1688 saw the last attempts to work the ancient constitution and ultimately the rapid disillusion of the gentry, the class which had the greatest political importance in England. In 1660 its extreme support of monarchy expressed the gentry's overwhelming desire for a restoration of that society in which it predominated, and even in the early 1680's the monarchy was still the barrier to republicanism and faction. In 1685 James II was thought to be a true Cavalier king. His reckless defiance of the most cherished principles of the class most loyal to him and his neglect of the constitutional balance which contained the real Restoration of 1660 forced the gentry to face squarely the issue of a legal conception of "absolutism" which was intolerable unless it was exercised for and not against the convictions of the gentry.

James II proved to the country the inadequacy of the traditional ways when "the true government of England (which) is founded in good measure upon a great confidence in the people" was impossible on account of the king's policy. The Divine Right of Kings ceased to be valid when the king, a Roman Catholic, challenged the national church. Trust in prerogative could not survive the governmental methods by which James promoted his policy. In 1688 as in 1641, England was "upon a nationall bottome", and, unlike 1641, the Church of England, united and disciplined, was able to accept a policy requiring concessions to dissent in order to isolate the king. The religious issue in 1688 did not produce a royalist party: religious disunion was accepted in order to preserve political co-operation against the king.

It was important that neither the Restoration nor the Revolution of 1688 was the work of extreme partisans. Although the years in between witnessed phases of acute tension, when, as in 1671, Charles II might have copied French absolutism, or, as in 1678, the proposal to exclude James, Duke of York, from the succession threatened civil war, it was the moderates who kept control of the Revolution when it came and prevented it from getting out of hand. The Revolution was not a Whig monopoly. The events of 1688 marked the rejection of the extreme doctrines formulated during the struggles of the past century. Divine right in any form lost its political significance. Republicanism was discredited. The attempt to have one exclusive church was abandoned.

Accompanying these changes in ideas, there was such a shift of power in the constitution as to settle decisively the relations between crown and parliament. The vague constitution and its confused precedents, inherited from the Middle Ages, modernized by the Tudors, and productive of fiercely contested interpretations, often radical, under the Stewarts, were defined so that the prerogative was not independent of the law as established by the King in Parliament. The legal theory that the king was "absolute" in government, though not the master of the lives and properties of his subjects, lost its hold when it became clear to the nation that the determination of public policy was the real issue. The co-operation of King and Parliament was the clamant need of seventeenth century politics. It had become obvious after 1660. In 1688 the crown lost the means to rule in opposition to parliament and this political fact set limits to the legal rights of the prerogative.

In Scotland, 1688 saw also the success of the moderates, and the beginning of a new period, following upon the freeing of secular activities from religious domination. Important as it was that the presbyterian church, with its own independent General Assembly, was finally established, it was of still greater importance that a free parliament, free from royal and ecclesiastical and one-party domination, and therefore a fit instrument of national policies, was at last secured. Behind these achievements was the acceptance of certain national ends as beyond controversy, however contested might be the means to bring them about.

Divine right, with its exclusive claims, was surrendered.

Not only was the Stewart claim to rule by divine right given up in favour of monarchy limited by law, but also the claims on behalf of the covenants, of the divine right of presbytery and of an intolerant national church were allowed to lapse. In Scotland, as in England, the more moderate attitude which had struggled throughout the century against extreme views at last prevailed, though adapted to new conditions; for it was not the impracticable idealism of Montrose, but the establishment of politically effective limitations on the crown which gave the answer. Parliament was recognized as the interpreter of the fundamental laws of the land, and its co-operation was essential in deciding policy. The Revolution in Scotland was the triumph of secular politics.

This outcome was the more notable because the Restoration in Scotland had been much more reactionary than in England. The political as well as the ecclesiastical work of the Covenanters was swept away. The monarchy was restored to its widest powers under James VI, and rapidly extended those powers. Episcopacy was restored more harshly than when it was introduced by James VI. The General Assembly was forbidden to meet. Parliament was only a little more independent than under James VI, and what resistance there was sprang from personal rather than public interest. The moderate presbyterians suffered for the excesses of the Covenanting remnant, provoked in part by the fears of a government which was too inefficient to ensure law and order. The majority of presbyterians were so cowed by the violence of the government and so alienated by the violence of the Covenanters and by the ruthless logic with which they interpreted Covenanting theory, that the majority was ready to thank James VII for his Indulgence of 1687.

Another reason for the comparative quiescence of the country was its poverty. It was only in the years immediately preceding the Revolution that Scotland had recovered from the exhaustion due to the Covenanters' crusades and to the occupation by Cromwell's army. The nobles especially had suffered, and after 1660 they failed to give leadership to the country. Other classes suffered on account of English economic and foreign policy after 1660. In 1688, therefore, the Scots were only able to take advantage of the opportunity offered by

English initiative in acting against James II. None the less, that opportunity was used as successfully as the English in 1640 had taken advantage of Scots' resistance to Charles I in 1638. It is this reversal of rôles which reveals most clearly the relations of the two countries between 1660 and 1688.

Criticizing the style of preaching in the Church of England after 1660 because of its appeal to state authority instead of to Scriptural argument, Lord Halifax pointed out that the "liberty of the late troubled times" had enlightened men and diffused so widely the appeal to discussion that the people were no longer to be dealt with as in an age of less inquiry. This was true in politics as much as in religion. The Restoration, the return to the constitutional position of 1641, was unable to obliterate the political education of the people induced by the challenges presented by civil wars and by the experience of the Protectorate. If the memory of Strafford's and Laud's policy of thorough was dimmed, the puritan version of it in Cromwell's government was generally obnoxious. The general desire to restore the traditional forms of government did not preclude an awareness of the significance of parliament, due to its unprecedented activity in the previous two decades. This mingling of the old and the new was effectively shown in the career of Hyde, Earl of Clarendon, the leading minister at the beginning of Charles II's reign.

From 1642, and during his exile with Charles II, Clarendon did not deviate from defending the full rights of monarchy according to law. He disliked the constitutional ideas of the extreme Anglicans and rejected any compromise with the presbyterians. He insisted that a stable settlement required that "the old banks be kept up". In 1660 he aimed at repairing "the old banks" of the law and at removing all recent obstacles to the stream of royal power within those banks. He had earlier weaned monarchy from the policy of thorough; he now successfully resisted a Cavalier reaction.

The Convention Parliament, which had restored Charles, now under Clarendon's lead worked out a settlement in accordance with the Declaration of Breda, issued by the king just before his return. The Act of Indemnity excluded only fifty persons, only two of whom were not involved in Charles I's execution. The settlement of the estates which had changed hands during the civil wars was moderate enough to win over the moderate puritans to the support of the crown. Those royalists who had disposed of estates by their own action obtained no satisfaction from the government; only the property of the king and queen, of the church and that of individuals which had been confiscated was restored.

The financial provision for the crown was less satisfactory: the army was paid off by special taxation, but the king's debts and that of the navy had to be met out of current revenue, which, in return for the king's surrender of his feudal dues, was to be made up by certain taxation granted to the king for life, and, with what remained of his hereditary revenues, was to amount to £1,200,000 annually. It was only after 1674 that a revival of trade gave to the king an adequate revenue. In the meantime, the financial question remained, as with the earlier Stewarts, to trouble Charles II's relations with parliament.

The Declaration of Breda had promised liberty to tender consciences and expressed the king's readiness to consent to an act of parliament granting that indulgence. The Convention Parliament dallied with a scheme of comprehension based on episcopacy as a presidency of synods. The king delayed any decision in order to allow public opinion to show itself. In 1661 the new—the Cavalier—parliament clearly expressed its strongly Anglican attitude. This was enough to doom the negotiations of episcopalians and presbyterians, although the latter had shown their own intolerance in discountenancing concessions to Roman Catholics and sectaries. It was in this same spirit that in the subsequent persecution the presbyterians refused to petition the king for a general indulgence, preferring that he alone should bear the responsibility of such a sin. The king's attempt in 1662 to obtain legislative sanction for the dispensing power inherent in himself came to nothing, and in 1663 a parliamentary committee held that a free parliament could not be bound by the Declaration of Breda. The king's indulgence was for Clarendon a matter of "ship money in religion", and one of the bishops told Charles that it meant "taking liberty to throw down the laws of the land at your pleasure".

Royalists and churchmen, whose alliance in 1642 on the basis of law enabled the king to fight, were once again allied, though this time to force their policy on the king. Churchmen were in 1662 as in 1688 the stoutest champions of parliament's constitutional claims, and parliament's policy was no less Erastian because it was less protestant. Consequently, while Laud's church triumphed in 1662, neither church nor state had room for another Laud. Ecclesiastics had little power over the laity after the Restoration apart from what the laity granted through parliament.

The religious legislation between 1661 and 1670, inspired in part by the violence of sectarian fanatics, ejected from the church all who refused episcopal ordination or the prayer book, excluded dissenters from office and professions, subjected dissenting preachers to great hardships and those who attended conventicles to severe penalties. By these means the gentry secured a firm hold over the towns, in which puritanism was strongest. Although dissent was now legally recognized in the sense that nonconformists were driven out of the established church, instead of the earlier policy of punishing those who did not attend its services, dissenters suffered from grave civil disabilities and were deprived of any security to worship in their own ways. Even more drastic proposals narrowly escaped being put upon the statute-book. Only the difficulty of enforcing these laws, the Indulgence of 1672 and the political rivalry of the Whig and Tory parties in the later years of the Cavalier parliament enabled dissent to endure and survive.

It was in his dealings with parliament that Clarendon showed himself out of touch with new needs. His ideal was that of 1641—of a king exercising his powers as a trust from God, advised by, and controlling administration through, the privy council, and in which parliament was "more or less or nothing" as he cared to make it. Clarendon refused to admit that the House of Commons was most qualified to judge of the necessities and grievances of the people and denied that the king's ministers should not offer advice which was opposed to the views of parliament. For the four years before his fall in 1667, Clarendon was disposed to use parliament as little as was necessary and even when the Dutch forced the Medway in

1667 he showed by his belief that the king and his counsellors alone were competent to meet the crisis how mistaken was his understanding of the new situation.

His neat division of executive and legislature, in which parliament shared the work of lawmaking, controlled taxation and initiated impeachments of ministers before the House of Lords, but was not to control government nor to dictate policy, depended upon a high degree of mutual confidence. The independent line taken by the Commons in matters of religion, of finance and of foreign policy proved that the fundamental question was once again the determination of public policy.

It was clear that the management of the aggressive Commons was the first task of the government. For this, there was need either of a strong monarchy capable of directing parliament and government, or of a strong ministry able to secure the cooperation of King and Parliament. The last alternative was possible only if it drew its strength from a predominant party; but parties were as yet only beginning to be formed. The fall of Clarendon in 1667 was the general recognition of the inadequacy of the system of 1641; the king had found that it was impossible "to do those things with the Parliament that must be done" without new ministers and methods.

The Restoration in Scotland was dominated by the effects of the military occupation by Cromwell's troops. In 1660, patriotism and the desire for national independence combined with the popularity of the Stewart dynasty to restore the monarchy, and also the unsolved problems of the relations of king, parliament and church which the conquest had not settled but ignored. Cromwell had triumphed before the reorientation of politics after Dunbar had proceeded very far. Consequently, the Restoration ended the frustration due to occupation but revived that due to internal antagonisms.

The lack of principles characteristic of Scotland after 1660 was largely due to the bewilderment of opinion on the crucial problems of the relations of church and state. The alternatives of covenant and erastian episcopacy, of covenanted and limited monarchy and unlimited monarchy by divine right, grim, unsatisfying and increasingly discredited alternatives, offered no constructive means to the evolution of a loyal presbyterianism.

The Covenant had been defeated at Dunbar and it never regained its hold, either by force or conviction. The monarchical reaction of 1660 was soon to reduce Scotland to a state of impotence and resentment. During the following twenty-eight years, the tragic experience of the country gave rise to a third way and forced Scots to modify their convictions. The new way required the tacit abandonment of the premises of political presbyterianism. The way to constitutionalism required a more secular conception of the state and the end of government by an extremist party.

The Union of Crowns complicated the Scottish settlement. As King of England, Charles had no need to fear Scotland. There was no longer a puritan party in England. He had the power to subdue Scotland. He himself told the discontented nobles that they could not dispense with monarchy without becoming a province of England. The danger of rebellion in 1666 was met in part by mobilizing the militia of the northern English counties. As an absentee king, Charles was free of Scottish opinion. He ruled through the privy council and by ministers such as the Earls of Middleton and Lauderdale. They were dependent on the king alone. So long as Scotland was quiescent, Charles was satisfied. His ministers had no need to be statesmen but only successful managers of parliament and people. Their success was to arouse in the opposition in both countries the fear that Charles' power as King of Scotland might be used to remove the restrictions on his government in England, and in the Exclusion crisis the possibility of civil war waged by the Stewarts as kings of Scotland was an important consideration.

The most serious consequence of the Union of Crowns was the way in which the King of England after 1660 had to take account of the needs and opinions of his larger, more populous and more prosperous kingdom. One instance of this was the re-introduction of episcopacy in the Scottish church in an unduly precipitate way. Episcopacy had been abolished since 1638, and many of the moderate royalist nobles, including Lauderdale, were averse to the restoration of their episcopal rivals. A letter of the king to the ministers of Edinburgh was understood to support presbyterianism.

The parliament of 1661—the "obsequious" parliament—by the Act Rescissory repealed all statutes from 1633 to 1649, and possibly to the Restoration. Thus, the acts of the 1641 parliament, to which Charles I had assented, were rescinded, unlike those of the English parliament in 1641, as well as those of the 1648 parliament which had adopted the Engagement. Legislation establishing presbyterianism was annulled but the Acts of the General Assemblies were still effective and presbyterianism continued on sufferance a little longer. By the Act anent Religion of 1661, the religious settlement was left to the king's discretion and in 1662 episcopacy was restored by the king's ecclesiastical supremacy. Clarendon had exerted himself to achieve this result.

This dubious restoration of episcopacy was made worse by the thoughtless enforcement by the privy council of a requirement that all ministers who had not obtained presentation by the patrons and collation by the bishops should be excluded from their churches. About a third chose ejection and began to minister to their flocks in the fields. Moreover, the new bishops were possessed of ecclesiastical power over synods and presbyteries to an extent which marked them off from James VI's bishops. To the fear of ecclesiastical autocracy was joined the political hatred of episcopacy as the instrument of royal absolutism.

There is much disagreement among historians as to whether a moderate presbyterian settlement was possible and workable in 1662, but there is general agreement that the religious policy of the government was provocative, short-sighted and executed in a deplorable manner.

The constitutional settlement approximated to the restoration of Charles I's government before 1636. The meeting of parliament after the Restoration was delayed till 1661 in order to control the elections. The need for an indemnity for the many who had accepted the English occupation reduced that parliament to subservience. An oath—later extended to the humblest officials—acknowledging the king as the only supreme governor, rejecting all foreign jurisdiction, and promising never to decline his authority, was prescribed. The Covenants were condemned. The prerogative was vindicated over appointments to offices, the militia, the summoning of parliament, and the declaration of peace and war. The Lords of the Articles were revived. No meetings of subjects were lawful without the king's express consent. All pretexts of disobedience on the grounds of religion or the king's interest were denounced. The king was granted an annual revenue of £40,000 and authorized to raise a considerable militia. In 1662 parliament ratified the ecclesiastical settlement. In 1663, it granted the right of the king to tax foreign articles at will, and renewed the election of the Lords of the Articles by bishops and nobles. Lauderdale claimed that the king was the absolute master in parliament. In the 1669 parliament he really nominated the Lords of the Articles, and Charles later recognized that they were "the securest fence of his government".

Charles had no such "fence" in England. From the outbreak of the war with the Dutch in 1665, foreign policy and finance embittered the relations of king and parliament. The question of ministerial responsibility was raised. Later, religion was linked to foreign policy, and the king had to face a serious challenge to his prerogative. The "country" party began to form out of those averse to court policies, and the constitutional struggle for power rapidly became the contest of parties, in itself a grave restriction of the freedom of the king to direct policy and control government.

The Restoration had not involved Charles in any commitments to foreign states, nor was he bound by the aggressive policies of the Commonwealth and Protectorate. The Dutch war 1651-3 had arisen out of many instances of commercial jealousy and maritime rivalry. Its outcome was to establish the traditions and strategy of the English navy which were continued after the Restoration. The Dutch were forced to agree to strike their flag in English seas and to compensate English losses in the earlier struggle in the Spice Islands. Sea-power was also able to compel Portugal to grant many privileges in amends for permitting her waters to be used by royalist ships in raids on English commerce.

When Cromwell found Spain unwilling to make the concessions he demanded for a war against France, Cromwell despatched in 1654 an expedition against the Spanish possessions in the West Indies, and secured Jamaica. In the resulting war, English fleets struck decisively at Spanish treasure fleets, and in the winter 1656-7 blockaded the Spanish coast. In 1657, England joined France in a campaign against Gravelines, Mardyke and Dunkirk, the last two, the one occupied in 1657 and the other in 1658, being handed over to English garrisons. By the end of the Protectorate, foreign policy was being criticized in terms of trading advantages and maritime opportunities. The war with Spain was becoming unpopular.

Charles II was able to end a war for which he lacked the means, and the country the interest, to pursue. Dunkirk was given up by Spain, and Jamaica remained in English hands, though without Spanish agreement. The enterprise of the Ironsides abroad ended with the reduction in the size of the standing army at the Restoration, and until the Revolution the problem of creating an army for service abroad without endangering liberties at home helped to prevent continental intervention by England. The Whig opposition in 1677 so distrusted the king that it preferred to intrigue with Louis XIV rather than to grant the means for Charles to oppose the French. The navy was to be the weapon to back English diplomacy, while commercial interests were strengthened by the participation of the court in the activities of the great trading companies.

Jealousy of the Dutch revived. There were many difficulties in the relations of the two countries, at sea and between their trading stations in the East Indies, in Africa and in North America. The commercial policy of the English government intensified rivalry. Charles' marriage with Catherine of Braganza in 1662 did not bring the advantages expected by an alliance with Portugal, struggling with French support against Spain. English friendship with France was balanced by the 1662 defensive alliance of the French and Dutch.

When war was declared in March 1665 against the Dutch, England had no important allies, and although Louis gave some aid to the Dutch, it was of small account. The real war was between the two great sea-powers—to the advantage of France. An English success off Lowestoft was counterbalanced by the failure to prevent De Ruyter from convoying a rich merchant fleet by northern waters to the Dutch ports. In 1666, the Dutch success in the Four Days' Battle in the Channel was later destroyed by the English victory off the North Foreland. In 1667 moves for a peace, due to the strain of war intensified by the ravages of the Plague and the Fire of London, and to Louis XIV's move against the Spanish Netherlands, were hastened by the bold stroke of the Dutch against the English fleet laid up in the Medway for reasons of economy. By the Treaty of Breda, 1667, England obtained the New Netherlands, and recognition of a salute to the English flag in the Channel. The Dutch obtained Surinam and Polaroon, and some modification of the English Navigation Laws.

The effects of this war were great at home. Its chequered course and inefficient organization stirred the Commons to further acts of constitutional aggression. In 1665 a grant of money was to be used only for the war—a move seen by the more conservative as "introductive to a Commonwealth". In 1667, the Commons made good a claim to investigate the financial side of the war, and the committee it appointed reported much mismanagement. Clarendon was made the scapegoat and went into exile to escape the consequences of the impeachment begun by his enemies. The king was free to deal with the leaders of the discontented Commons, but without admitting the idea of ministerial responsibility. The effects of the war on future foreign policy tended to divide king and people. To the king, the lesson was to avoid a policy opposed to France, though not necessarily to adopt active collaboration: to the people the fear of the Dutch was gradually overshadowed by the growing might of France, especially as an economic competitor.

The years of the "Cabal", the five political adventurers in the service of the king, lacking principles but loving power, opposed to Clarendon's policy and to the Anglican church, and not even united among themselves, were the years in which Charles made his own policy that of the government. He was testing the opinion of the country and bidding for its support. He attempted to unify the political direction by giving a strong lead, the success of which, it was hoped, would increase the king's prestige at the expense of parliament. A strong monarchy seemed the only alternative to the existing political confusion arising out of the assertiveness of parliament, its distrust of the government, and the pressure, prejudiced and ignorant very often, clumsily exerted on the executive.

If Clarendon's system was out of date, the blundering Commons needed to be managed unless a consistent and rational policy was to be abandoned; for with only the rudiments of party, the Commons were unfitted to initiate policy. Moreover, the king's experiences of the bigotry, the narrow economic policies, and class interests of his parliament led him to see his policy as more enlightened and more suitable for a modern society. Hence, his inclination to catholicism which meant, politically, government from above, and, socially, order and tradition. The restoration of Roman catholicism was necessary for the restoration of his prerogative, and the reduction of parliamentary and popular influence on government. From 1667 to 1673 there was the experiment of independent royal government; thereafter, Charles had to take account of parties.

There were three important stages in the experiment. First, Charles allied himself with Louis XIV by the Treaties of Dover 1670. The secret treaty provided help for the conversion of England at the time Charles deemed best. The open treaty, known to the protestant as well as the catholic members of the Cabal, was for a war to partition Dutch territories. Secondly, after parliament was prorogued in 1671 for two years, Charles appealed to public feeling by the issue of a Declaration of Indulgence through the king's prerogative. Protestant dissenters were to be allowed public worship on certain conditions, and Roman Catholics were permitted to worship in private houses. Thirdly, the Dutch war which began in 1672 was designed to give swift and complete victory. England was to land troops on the Dutch coast, while the French launched the main attack by land. By defensive strategy at sea and by flooding the inland provinces, the Dutch checked the danger to their independence. For Charles, the unsuccessful gamble of an easy and overwhelming victory ended his experiment in personal rule. In 1673, he had to summon parliament to obtain grants for the war, and to submit to the terms parliament demanded.

Behind the Scottish rebellions of 1666 and 1679 was the

political theory of the covenants which retained its political vitality long after revolutionary ideas had almost disappeared in England. The aim of this theory was to justify the policy of the covenanters in victory or in defeat, to justify, that is to say, the fearless destruction of all resistance to government by covenanters and also their own resistance to any other kind of government. After 1660 when the work of the covenanters was destroyed by Charles II's ministers, it was necessary to defend resistance to the existing government; but since presbyterians were divided among themselves, the nobles supported Charles and parliament was a royal instrument, it was equally necessary to appeal to the true source of authority and obedience.

The militant covenanters were in a minority, and could not appeal to democratic arguments, to the people at large and to the representatives of the people, without claiming first that they were the people and secondly that all human power was strictly subject to God's law. The king, parliament, nobles, and majority of the people were to be obeyed in so far as they upheld that Law. Private persons had a duty to God to secure universal obedience to His Law, and a right against their fellow-men so to act, a right which was inalienable and indestructible, to be defended against any human authority which ruled contrary to God's Law. Violent resistance to persons of whatever degree or number using force to govern contrary to that Law was called for by the Law itself.

Human will had no part in the Law except to will on earth what was ordained in heaven. Therefore, all pretexts of conscience and of interpretation, roads to anarchy in church and state, were dismissed. The principle that a man's own conscience was the only warrant and ground of his submission or non-submission, or of his obedience or disobedience, was expressly repudiated. No man was bound by his "erring" conscience; nor was his conviction of being injured in the true religion a sufficient ground for resistance. The claim to defend the true religion did not justify any sect using force to defend what it took to be the true religion.

The individual conscience had a peculiar place in covenanting thought. It was the final authority for a man. If a people fell from grace and granted to a government a power to command sin, it was an invalid grant for the people to make; no men and no body of men could authorize sin. Nobody could loose the obligation of God's Law. Nobody could take away the right of self-defence, that is of protecting individual freedom to act in conformity to the Law, even though a majority of people failed to enforce this right. The individual conscience had the right to judge what was the Law, but this did not justify whatever was thought to be right. Clearly the covenanters were claiming to be right and that all other men had no right other than to admit this.

The elaborate political theory of the *Jus Populi Vindicatum*, defending the rebellion of 1666, was determined by this peculiar appeal to the conscience. The dependence of king and parliament on the people, who had an innate power of self-defence, the nature of government as a trust or a fiduciary power, the justification of government as means to preserve people's rights and to provide a better state than had existed previously, the subordination of the supreme power, even in democracy, to the people's safety, all of which were current during the Civil Wars, were distorted by the Covenanters' conception of "the people". The people was the body of men whose consciences rightly discerned and obeyed God's Law. It was essentially a self-constituted body and therefore bound to use force against all who differed from it.

In England, the difficulty of deciding which conscience was right, which interpretation of God's Law was right, had stimulated theories of toleration and of a secular state which influenced the attitude of dissenters after the Restoration and moderated their extremism. It was among some of the politically minded Whigs that a claim of a minority to be the people was defended, but it was more difficult to justify a policy of forcing men to be free by a rational law of nature than to defend, as the Covenanters did, the duty of the Elect to rule the nation.

The defence of the Scottish government against the rebels was made by Sir George Mackenzie. It was natural that he denied the right of "the juster or better part" of the people to act as the people, but his own thought was bound by the outmoded legal argument of the prerogative. The king of Scotland is an "absolute" king, unlimited by any human power, under no coercive law, and drawing his authority wholly from God. The king has no right to dispose of "our estates", for property is the subjects' birthright and what was once "ours" cannot be taken away without "our" consent. Monarchy is a government and can include no more than what is necessary for government, but the king is as free to regulate all matters of government as "we" are to regulate "our" property, for government is the king's property. Everything necessary for government pertains to the king, even without any definite law, provided that he does not act contrary to the laws of God, Nature and Nations.

It was unlawful for the king to force religion by use of arms, instead of argument. Equally it was unlawful for a king, with or without parliament, to act against the fundamental laws of the kingdom or to rule arbitrarily against the higher laws. Parliament was entitled to secure legal protection of the nation's religion and laws from any successor to the throne, and no statute was repealable without parliamentary consent.

James VII's reign was to be a convincing proof that the lawyer's case was as unreasonable as the covenanters, and the self-limitation of Stewart monarchy as worthless as the claim of the juster part of the people to limit government. Meanwhile, the period between the two rebellions was dominated by Lauderdale, whose frank Erastianism, expressed in the Assertory Act of 1669, checked the indiscreet zeal of the Archbishops' party and offered the Indulgence to such of the deprived ministers as were willing to minister to their parishioners without resisting the episcopal organization of the church. The Indulgence was extended in 1672. The west was more peaceable but the Eastern Lowlands began to copy the west country's nonconformity in order to gain the benefits of Indulgence. The Indemnity of 1674 was interpreted to be a sign of favour, and conventicles and field preaching spread rapidly.

Lauderdale's policy of conciliation only encouraged presbyterians. He had cause to fear the large conventicles, "brought to resemble armies", in which "ministers preacht whatever was their own opinion in any emergent case; the people were as much judges as disciples". Young field preachers entered into competition with the indulged ministers and sought to undermine their ministry. Even presbyterians warned Lauderdale of the danger of rebellion. He had neither the forces nor the political machinery for effective repression without cruelty and arbitrary acts; equally, fear of the English High Church party prevented concessions likely to achieve a lasting settlement. Hence the alternations of excessive rigour and undue relaxation of laws against presbyterians which were deplored by Leighton, the most understanding and forbearing of Scottish bishops.

In 1677 Lauderdale took stern measures to anticipate the danger of a more or less chance union of the large, armed conventicles, only too likely to evoke in their leaders violent expressions of enthusiastic fanaticism. To force landowners to become responsible for their tenants, and to suppress conventicles, Highlanders were quartered upon the gentry of the south-west. In 1678 a tax for the support of troops against conventicles added to the unrest. In 1679 the murder of Sharp, Archbishop of St. Andrews, and the clash of soldiers and conventicles in the south-west, produced rebellion. In the Rutherglen declaration the authority of the persecuting government was virtually renounced. A skirmish on the moors at Drumclog ended in the retreat of the soldiers under Graham of Claverhouse.

Glasgow had to be evacuated, but the rebels quarrelled bitterly among themselves. The extremists would fight with none who did not repudiate the Indulgence and held that Charles had forfeited the authority accorded by the Covenants. The moderates declared their aims to be the defence of protestantism and presbyterian church government, the preservation of the king's lawful authority in accordance with true religion and the kingdom's liberties, and the calling of a free parliament and free assembly. Thus divided, the rebels were crushed at Bothwell Bridge by the Duke of Monmouth. Most of the victims of justice refused to save themselves by a pledge never to rise in arms again, although a meeting of some presbyterian ministers deemed the pledge lawful. Monmouth obtained the Third Indulgence suspending the acts against house—but not field—conventicles in the area south of the Tay.

Bothwell Bridge was the doom of the covenants. Another rebellion was impossible. The excesses of the extremists had alienated the moderate presbyterians. The covenants were identified with the theocracy of a few unenlightened zealots on behalf of a minority, and their violence and intolerance led the majority to the humble hope that their faith might be allowed on sufferance. The episcopal church had prevailed: its later collapse was due to James VII's policy of a catholic restoration. But the episcopal church was not Laudian. Its forms of worship had continued almost presbyterian; its presbyteries and synods survived; its bishops were without the power and status of English bishops. Erastianism had neutralized divine right. The related problem of the prerogative which had troubled Scottish politics throughout the century, however, remained unsettled.

In England, the prerogative, mingled with issues of religion and foreign policy, was hotly disputed from 1673–81, and the settlement of 1688, though not its spirit, was anticipated in the Exclusion controversy. The two sessions of parliament in 1673, necessary to obtain supplies for the Dutch war, not only resulted in far-reaching legislation but also in a considerable threat to the prerogative. The House of Lords held that toleration must be in a parliamentary way. The Commons insisted on the Test Act before supplies. By this act, containing a declaration against transubstantiation, which no catholic could take, all office-holders had to join in the sacrament of the Lord's Supper according to Anglican practice. This simple test, exclusive and intolerant, became the main defence of Anglicanism in church and state.

To Halifax in more difficult times, the Test Act and the Habeas Corpus Act of 1679 were the guarantees of protestantism and parliament. Charles had to cancel the Indulgence. There were suggestions in the Commons that certain of its addresses to the king might be published. In October 1673, parliament protested against James' second marriage to a catholic, and against "evil councillors", and threatened to grant no further supplies until further measures against catholics were taken. In the following January, bills were proposed against illegal imprisonment, and illegal exaction of money, and for the education of James' children as protestants.

The naval war during 1673 proved that the Dutch were able to prevent an English landing and the battle of the Texel ended the blockade of Dutch ports. Peace was made in February 1674 on the basis of a salute to the English flag as a mark of respect, a small indemnity, and a concession with regard to the law of neutrality at sea. During the next four years, while the Dutch and French were still at war, England gained in trade and maritime development.

Charles' experiment in personal government having collapsed, he had to find some way of working with parliament without sacrificing the prerogative in the essential duties of monarchy. The "constitutional negations" of Clarendon had also broken down. It was necessary to restore parliament's confidence in the king in order to secure its co-operation, without which government was paralysed. Mutual confidence would have given to the king the active support of parliament and the opportunity to guide its growing power; but only provided that the king voluntarily confined his freedom to determine policy by respecting the dearest convictions of his parliament. The prerogative was likely to survive only if it was popular. The issue of the responsibility for deciding public policy once again was raised by the alternatives of policy before the nation.

Charles found in the Earl of Danby a minister conscious of the issue and of the way it ought to be met; but the king continued his own secret policy despite his minister, compelled Danby to further it, and destroyed the confidence of parliament in the king, to restore which had been Danby's purpose. The opposition in 1673 was due to the fear of France, popery and arbitrary government. The last meant the methods by which the king aimed at the first two. Danby held that fear of the methods would endure only in the minority headed by the Earl of Shaftesbury, earlier a member of the Cabal, a supporter of the Indulgence and of the Dutch war, but no party to a catholic revival and, therefore, a supporter of the Test Act, provided that fear of the ends of Charles' policy—France and popery—was removed.

A letter of Danby to the king outlined the issues. The king could never be great nor rich till he "fall into the humour of the people". The prerogative was in danger unless the king could rule without parliaments, which the condition of the revenues prevented. He could not hope to rule by force. Parliament would not help unless the French policy was abandoned. The present parliament, "than wch. I never hope to see a better", was resolved to meet often and expected the king's gratitude for making up the deficiency in his revenue.

Danby had a clear and consistent programme. On the one hand, by stringent financial control he hoped to take advantage of the improving conditions of trade and the yield from the customs to make the king eventually independent of parliamentary grants, and so to eliminate the dangerous alternative of parliamentary control of policy. He was unable to achieve this aim, partly because of the king's ways, and was more dependent on parliament than he had intended. On the other hand, he tried to build up a great party in parliament on the basis of church and crown, and of an Anglican monopoly of power, by the exclusion of all who did not subscribe to Anglican principles from public office, parliament and local government.

By a new Test he proposed that an oath against resistance to the king and against the alteration of the laws in church and state should be imposed on officials, justices of the peace and members of parliament. The country party would have been driven out of political and official life, and England would have been reduced to the restless impotence behind Scottish public life. Danby admired Lauderdale and his system of government. Danby's Test failed owing to a dispute between the House of Lords and House of Commons. Shaftesbury's opposition to the Test marks the clear beginning of another great party in opposition to Danby. Shaftesbury appealed to the gentry to beware of the prerogative, called on the opposition to make terms with dissent, demanded the election of a new House of Commons, since a standing parliament as much as a standing army was against national interests.

Danby wanted a foreign policy—a Dutch alliance and commercial agreement with Spain—which would be popular. In this the king did not co-operate. Louis XIV wanted English neutrality and was willing to subsidize Charles to prevent parliament forcing Charles into war against France. In 1677, parliament pressed for war but refused grants until a Dutch alliance was concluded. Again Charles agreed with Louis to delay the next session of parliament in return for a subsidy. At the end of the year Charles agreed to the marriage of William of Orange and Mary, James' elder daughter, partly to allay an excited public at home and partly to force Louis to hasten the conclusion of peace. Charles posed to parliament as a patriot king. Parliament made grants with strict appropriation to the war. Louis was able to play upon the suspicions of the opposition and to excite dread of Charles' use of the army which had been raised. Until Louis finally made peace in 1678 with Spain and the Netherlands, Charles played a dangerous game with Louis and with parliament, obtaining money but retaining independence of policy.

The Popish Plot, the grimly grotesque invention of Titus Oates, produced panic and the Cavalier Parliament yielded to its influence. In its last months it attacked the king's ministers, his control of the army and James' place in the king's councils. It excluded all catholics, except James, from parliament. The disclosure of Danby's unwilling share in Charles' relations with Louis led to Danby's impeachment, and the dissolution of parliament. Danby's failure caused the odium of popery and France to remain with the Tories—his party of church and crown—until 1688. His programme of exclusive Anglicanism and independent prerogative was undermined by the catholic policy of the king.

The elections to the new parliament marked the emergence of party organization and programme. The opposition urged the electors to judge the records of the late members, to ignore courtiers and placemen, to choose protestants and those who would advocate frequent parliaments and relaxation of laws against the dissenters. The king could only rely on thirty members in the new parliament. James left England, Danby was sent to the Tower; a new council to transact business and composed of both parties, with Shaftesbury as president, was established, and a bill to exclude James from the succession passed its second reading in the Commons.

On this last point, Charles was adamant: he would not surrender the principle of hereditary monarchy. Shaftesbury was dismissed and parliament dissolved. Charles had two more parliaments, one which met in November 1680, and the other in April 1681. In both, the crucial issue was that of exclusion. The Whig party used its majorities against the Tories in imitation of Danby's policy. It gravely weakened its cause by supporting the Duke of Monmouth's claim to the crown instead of that of William of Orange, who was unlikely to be a party tool. The refusal to consider the expedient of limitations upon the monarchy for the protection of protestantism, which moderates like Halifax advocated and many Tories were prepared to accept, and which constituted definite restrictions of the prerogative, drove the moderates and Tories to support the king. The Whigs were extremists, determined to obtain a monopoly of political power and a puppet king.

The exclusion dispute presented to the nation a clear-cut and simple issue transcending personal and provincial interests and dividing the nation along party lines. The moderates were forced to choose one side or the other, and did not form a third party. In the debates of these years, the Whigs developed the principles which were to form the 1688 settlement. The aim was to remove the king's opportunities of governing against the wishes of his subjects, to ensure that public policy was determined by parliament, and that the prerogative was confined by the rights of property.

In effect, the Whigs were claiming that parliament must accept the ultimate responsibility for government. Hence, the demands for frequent parliaments, ministerial responsibility, independent judges, the exclusion of placemen, no army without parliamentary consent, and the punishment of illegal taxation as high treason. Extreme as these principles were, there was no trace of the radical doctrines of the civil war. The Whigs trod the narrow way of the common law tradition. Theories and slogans of contract, consent and natural rights lost much of their terrors. The 1688 settlement was the more peaceable because debated so vigorously a decade earlier.

The extremism of the Whigs alienated the country. The fear of civil war, in which Scotland, Ireland and France were likely to aid the king, united the Tories and Crown, and rallied the moderates or Trimmers like Halifax to their support. By his skilful tactics, Charles had saved the prerogative and made it appear as the barrier to revolution. In the last parliament of 1681, he was able to pose as the champion of legality.

The loyalty of the Tories was more than recovered by Charles. By their conduct in the last stages of the Cavalier parliament, they had prepared the way for the Whigs and had discovered too late how great was the threat to their interests as well as to their convictions. The House of Commons was discredited. It needed to be transformed into a Tory stronghold. Danby's policy needed to be revived and for this they turned to the king as the unconditional leader of their party.

In their panic, and because they had not worked out any political doctrine as logical as the Whigs, the result of their refusal to consider that a catholic king would dare or be able to overthrow the Church of England, the Tories relied upon the divine right of kings, indefeasible hereditary right, the religious duty of non-resistance, the blasphemous character of criticism of the king, and the absolute and paternal nature of government. In this the Tories delivered themselves to the divines and forsook the lawyers. It was at this time that Filmer's *Patriarcha*, the most reasonable attempt to expound the divine right of kings, was published, and its popularity is in itself evidence that the Tories were seeking a rational explanation of their convictions.

Probably these exaggerations were only superficial. A Jacobite tract of 1693 dismisses them very coolly: "tho some Men have disputed warmly for the Natural and Patriarchal Right of Kings, yet they have so few Followers, and the Hypothesis itself is so new, and built upon such uncertain Conjectures, and so contrary to plain Matter of Fact, and the universal practice of all Nations, that it is not worth any man's contending about". Nor was non-resistance the fantastic conception of minds blinded by romantic loyalty. No thinker and politician was more clear-sighted than Halifax. In the crisis of 1687, he declared that "we are not to be laughed out of our passive obedience and the doctrine of non-resistance, though even those who perhaps owe the best part of their security to that principle are apt to make a jest of it". The Trimmer is proof that reason was not all on one side.

Danby's policy had been to eliminate the Whig and dissenting cause, and to contain the court and catholics by the power of parliament. Charles himself did not call another parliament but by his preparations he ensured that James should deal with a loyal and Tory House of Commons. The Whigs helped to destroy themselves by their implication in the Rye House plot (1683). The king was able to use the judges to break down the liberties within which Whiggery lurked. The attack upon the towns— the strongholds of Whigs and dissent—by finding legal pretexts for the forfeiture of the charters placed the government of the towns under the influence of the local gentry. The political balance of town and country was redressed in favour of the country. The gentry, now Anglican, reasserted the political control of their puritan grandfathers over the boroughs, and in English history it was the gentry who proved the staunchest bulwark against despotism. Moreover, the Rye House plot justified the removal of Whigs from the offices of local government in the counties—the Lord Lieutenancies and Justices of the Peace—and from the militia.

Charles' revenge had done much to consolidate the hold of the gentry on parliament and local government. The result was obvious in James' parliament—"such a landed parliament (was) never seen"—but still more in James' attempts to reverse the Tory triumph and end the Tory hold over both parliament and local government. Charles left to his brother a prerogative almost intact in spite of the troubles of his reign, but it rested on the faith of the Tory party. The Tories assumed that prerogative and party would work together for the advantage of each. James forced them to recognize that the prerogative was dangerous to themselves and to their cause.

James II was determined "not to reign precariously" and declared that to aim at frequent parliaments "by doles of supplies" was a very improper method to take with him. At first he thought that the Church of England under his strong lead would acquiesce in his catholic policy but later he admitted that "Church of England men were his only enemies". A moderate policy on his part would have obtained reasonable liberties for Roman Catholics, but he was so elated by the suppression of Monmouth's rebellion in 1685 that he aimed at presenting to parliament his policy as an accomplished fact through the executive power and upheld by the judges. He prorogued parliament when it was disinclined to repeal the Test and Habeas Corpus Acts. He used the dispensing power to introduce Roman Catholics into the army which had been used against Monmouth and was now to intimidate London. In Ireland, Roman Catholics controlled the army and government. The fleet was under a Roman Catholic admiral. Popish institutions and offices were revived.

The Church of England was given cause to fear by the creation of a court of Commissioners, contrary to the Act of 1641, to exercise the ecclesiastical supremacy of the crown. The court suspended Compton, Bishop of London, for failing to discipline his clergy, and helped the king to introduce Roman Catholics into the Universities. In 1687, James issued the first Declaration of Indulgence, liberal in spirit, but removing the constitutional safeguard of the Test Act. He still hoped for toleration in a parliamentary way by influence on corporations and local government to support representatives committed to the repeal of the Test Act. The Tory nobles led the general refusal to agree.

In 1688, a Second Declaration of Indulgence was ordered to be read in every parish church. Seven of the episcopate petitioned against it. Resistance to the wrong doing of ministers was not resistance to the king, it was argued. The bishops felt that not to protest against the Indulgence was to countenance the election of a parliament for the repeal of the Test Act. For daring "to pretend that reasons might be offered to justify disobedience", the bishops were tried for publishing a seditious slander, and acquitted. Tories and Whigs turned to William of Orange as their only means to check James. It was fortunate that William had need of the English alliance, and still more that Louis XIV committed his armies in Germany. William's bold landing and circumspect waiting on events was in contrast to James' indecision and childish flight in the hope that England would disintegrate. The issue of the prerogative was at last decided, and James had converted almost the whole country to settle it in a peaceable and sensible manner.

In Scotland, as in England, after 1680, the power of the crown seemed unrestrained; its enemies were small and insignificant groups of extremists, and parliament was made up of loyal supporters. By 1688, James' religious policy had alienated parliament and episcopalians, without gaining the loyalty of the presbyterians.

The bulk of the people had acquiesced in an established church nominally episcopalian but free of the extremes which in 1638 had caused resistance. The government's fears of the extremists led to measures by which moderate men suffered. The extreme Covenanters, now organized in local societies and meeting in United Societies, formed a state within the state, separated from all who would not agree to all their principles, and in the Sanquhar Declaration of 1680 disowned Charles as king, because he had rejected the covenants, maintained prelacy and Erastianism, permitted idolatry and persecuted men for maintaining the Lord's right to rule consciences. This remnant claimed to be the true presbyterian church and the covenanted nation, and to have the divine right to establish its authority over both. It declared war against all who did not repudiate the authority of the state. The king and his ministers were excommunicated. The government feared that the extremists were prepared for violent acts, even of assassination, and used torture to elicit proof of such intentions. Many were executed for refusing to disavow the lawfulness of killing the king and his servants.

James had retired to Scotland as the king's representative to avoid provocation to the Whigs during the Exclusion controversy. In the parliament of 1681 he was able to ensure his succession to the Scottish throne by an act which affirmed the principle of hereditary right whatever the religion of the heir. A Test Act to exclude opponents from office and parliament and to apply to all dissenters was passed. At first, it was intended to be an oath to maintain the true protestant religion, but the king obtained the inclusion of his supremacy in both civil and ecclesiastical matters, the repudiation of the covenants and the right to take up arms, and the denial of any right to meet without the king's consent.

To counteract these clauses the true protestant religion was explained as that given in John Knox's *Confession*, now forgotten and impossible to be reconciled to the king's clauses. Opportunity was thus given for a good deal of obstruction and interpretation, but if the privy council had to make concessions to the episcopal viewpoint, offence was given to moderate presbyterian sentiment by the terms of the Test, and still more by the fact that immunity from the increasing pressure of the government's regulations to reduce the extremists depended upon taking the offensive Test. A proclamation empowered the Privy Council to question any who had contact in any way, by accident or not, with the rebels of 1679, whether legally condemned or not.

The government was acting against abettors and sympathisers of the extremists, but in an intolerably inquisitorial way. Meanwhile, Claverhouse struck at all who refused the bond to keep the peace and at the leaders of the conventicles, by such means filling the parish churches. In 1684 the last fanatical revival of conventicles under Renwick, who was in 1688 the last Covenanting martyr, led to the publication of his Apologetical Declaration in which the enemies of the Cause and all who aided those enemies were to be punished in due manner. Outrages against indulged ministers followed. The government retorted by an oath of Abjuration of the clause in the Apologetical Declaration declaring war against the king. Summary execution awaited any who refused the oath in the presence of two witnesses. No one was permitted to travel without a certificate of such Abjuration.

James VII inherited the throne in 1685. Parliament was intensely loyal, granting the excise permanently to the crown, placing on men between the ages of sixteen and sixty years the duty to serve the king wherever he directed, punishing attendance at conventicles with death and applying the Test to protestant landowners. Presbyterianism was prostrate, the government subservient and James insistent on freeing Roman Catholics from penal laws as well as to protect them by the law. Their worship was publicly allowed and there were conversions among the king's ministers.

In 1686, however, parliament proved that no class was willing to aid the king in abolishing the penal laws. It was prepared to admit Roman Catholic worship in private, but not to open offices of every kind to papists. The bishops were against such a step. So were the boroughs, managed as the elections had been,—"the burrows were the brazen wall the

Papists found hardest"—and they were supported by the shire representatives. Parliament was adjourned to prevent the rejection of the government's measure. The laity's fear of Roman Catholicism had given determination to a packed parliament to thwart a strong king. Local and sectional interests were overcome by national feeling. Parliament, the secular representative of the nation, expressed public opinion.

James made it clear that he did not need parliamentary co-operation, and suspended the penal laws by virtue of his ecclesiastical supremacy. Roman Catholics enjoyed worship in public, but presbyterians in 1687 were at first only allowed to worship in private and the ministers had to take an oath of non-resistance. This last requirement was soon abandoned, and by the third Letter of Indulgence the presbyterians were allowed to worship in chapels under certain safeguards of public order. The main resistance to James had sprung from the episcopalians: the proud spirit of the covenants did not survive nearly three decades of repression. A more secular spirit was then possible in Scotland, and therefore sufficient tolerance to allow the growth and activity of several parties. The essential conditions for constitutional government were at last acceptable to the nation.

CHAPTER VI

THE UNION OF 1707

IN less than twenty years after the Revolution of 1688, England and Scotland abandoned the earlier Union of the Crowns in favour of an incorporating union in which a separate Scottish parliament was deliberately allowed no place. The Union of 1707 was the outcome of the plain needs of both countries, and of negotiations in which hard bargaining and party politics played their part. A new awareness of Scottish national interests was fostered by English indifference to the political claims, and by its hostility to the economic competition, of Scotland. Fortunately for the Union, England, once aroused to the possibility of separation, was ready at last to treat Scotland as an equal, although taking care to show the wisdom of sharing its markets and of avoiding a challenge to its military power.

The Revolution enabled Scotland to adopt a more independent attitude towards England. So long as the Stewarts' claim to the throne was conceded, Scotland was not only tied to England, but also was unable to limit the powers of its kings. William's success provided the opportunity for a Convention of Estates in 1689 to offer the crown upon certain political conditions, although the failure to demand economic concessions by England at the same time was subsequently regretted. The Jacobites in the Convention were paralysed by James' insistence on his rights, and Claverhouse's bold bid to raise the Highlanders against William lost its force after his own death in the hour of victory at Killiecrankie.

The Convention's work was carried out by a solid party resolutely opposed to Stewart misrule. There was no need to qualify the reasons for deposing James. He was declared to have forfeited the throne because he had evaded the Coronation Oath "to maintain the Protestant Religion and to rule the people according to the Laudable Laws", and because he had sought to convert the government "from a legal limited monarchy to an arbitrary despotic power". The aim of the Convention was to condemn the system of government since the Restoration and to prevent for the future a strong monarchy resting upon "obsequious" parliaments.

The offer of the Crown to William and Mary was joined to the Claim of Right and a list of grievances, in which James' illegal acts were condemned as contrary to law, episcopacy was declared a "great and insupportable grievance and trouble to this Nation and contrary to the inclinations of the generality of the people", and frequent and free parliaments were demanded. Under the guise of rights and grievances, the Convention secured a parliamentary constitution after the English pattern, and the conditions imposed on the crown secured its dependence on parliament.

When the Convention became a parliament, extremists attempted to use the new parliamentary powers to reduce the executive to the dependence of 1641, and there was general determination to abolish the Lords of the Articles in order to exclude royal control over parliamentary activities. William was anxious to retain the Lords of the Articles to facilitate the constructive co-operation of the government with parliament. The first session of parliament was rendered almost sterile by these disputes and by the predominance of the sectional interests and oligarchical spirit which had prevented effective parliamentary opposition to Charles II and James VII. In the next session of 1690, William agreed to the abolition of the Lords of the Articles. The extremists were discredited by their self-seeking intrigues with the Jacobites. The king's ministers gained some influence over parliament and the result was seen in important measures of reconstruction, especially the establishment of the Presbyterian church. Learning to use its power for national ends and to influence rather than to obstruct the government, parliament became at last "the real arbiter of the destinies of the nation", and by its legislative action "substantially governed".

The establishment of presbyterianism closed the struggle over divine right in church and state. From 1690, the General Assembly met annually and exercised the greatest influence on the nation. The presbyterian ideal of the co-operation of the civil and ecclesiastical powers had triumphed at the same time that a limited monarchy had ended the claims of the prerogative. The relations of church and state were open to more rational treatment when the church had to face a national representative of secular affairs. The differences between the political and ecclesiastical parliaments had not the same emotional appeal as the contest of King Christ and King Stewart. The moderation of the church was noteworthy. The Covenants were allowed to fall into obscurity and there was less desire to interfere in politics, so that politicians were able to evade the problem of limiting the church to religious matters only. The church, indeed, had no alternative to the Revolution Settlement and had to adjust its claims to the rise of parliament and of secular interests.

In England, the Revolution was the work of two parties, and the immediate settlement of the throne, together with William's concessions during his reign, provided the national framework within which the parties were to develop. The Whigs expected William to be their tool but even though he proved too strong for that, their position prevented them from pursuing their normal programme of limiting the crown because the success of the Revolution depended upon William. The Tories were long reluctant to accept as final the break in the Stewart succession, which meant the breakdown of their bid for a political monopoly based on the Church of England, but if the fear of a Roman Catholic king, forced on the country by French arms, was acute enough to hold their loyalty to the Revolution, they had no inclination to uphold the prerogative of a king of foreign birth.

The attitude of both parties was modified after 1688. This was assisted by one consequence of the Revolution—the reversal of foreign policy and the war with France. Until 1697 England was part of William's Grand Alliance against Louis XIV and engaged in a hard and unrewarding struggle. Although the needs of war compelled William to make concessions to parliament, the threat to the Revolution settlement set limits to party encroachment on the crown.

The Revolution was interpreted as an extraordinary

measure to preserve the law and to reduce the prerogative to its just limits. The Convention of 1689, intended to prepare the way for a legal parliament, declared that James had threatened the laws and religion of the country through his evil advisers, and that his flight amounted to abdication. Many of the Tories accepted the view that James had deserted his subjects, but those who would not abjure him clung to the idea of a regency.

William's attitude made it necessary to offer the crown to him and to his wife on the conditions given in a Declaration of Rights, the basis of the Bill of Rights, closing the gaps in the system of government which had allowed the later Stewarts to rule in spite of the lack of co-operation of crown and parliament, and brought the legal doctrine of the prerogative into line with the law as declared by King in Parliament. Since 1661 parliament had become more active: after 1688 the need of supplies, due to war, necessitated annual meetings of parliament, with the result that the struggle for predominance in the composite body declaring law was decided in favour of parliament. The year 1688 was more than a logical development of the constitutional claims of 1641; in the course of the struggle, parliament had acquired a new appreciation of its authority.

William was willing to work with both parties, and constructed his cabinets out of those elements willing to support his foreign policy in return for reasonable concessions. His ministers were responsible to him and did not depend upon the support of parliament. He personally controlled both the war and foreign policy. The initiation of, and responsibility for, policy was still the king's, but it was necessary for him to gain the support of parliament, the weapon of which continued to be obstruction. The king's ministers had to "manage" the Commons by every kind of inducement.

The king's critics tried to extend the control of parliamentary committees over the administration, were suspicious of placemen (those in the Commons who held offices from the king), were anxious to separate the executive and legislature, and aimed at making king and ministers the creatures of parliament. These critics insisted on the pre-Revolution principle "that the king has his council to advise with established by law, and that in Corners and Chambers is not our Council of England".

The Privy Council was to be responsible to parliament for royal government. To Halifax the war was a practical expedient much more effective than the speculative and controverted principle of divine right to extract supply. " 'Twill look like a Parliament of Paris; the king to propose, and they to verify it", another declared, if parliament has to grant whatever was asked for the war.

William had to agree in 1694 to the Triennial Act by which new elections were to take place every three years. The Commons were careful to see that money grants were expended by the king in accordance with the terms and purpose of the grants. After the peace with France in 1697, a Tory parliament was able to curtail the king's powers and by the Act of Settlement, 1701, to provide for the Hanoverian Succession on conditions restricting the crown still more. The new royal line was to conform to the Church of England; to leave England, Scotland and Ireland only with parliamentary consent; to have officials of English parentage; and to be allowed the use of English forces in defence of continental possessions only upon parliamentary approval. The other clauses prevented the king from controlling the judges and ending the impeachment of his ministers by a pardon under the Great Seal.

The strength and continuity of the English settlement of 1688 was due to the initial compromise between the Tories and the Whigs. The Tories had contradicted their theories by opposing James and agreeing to William's succession. Divine hereditary right was discredited. Non-resistance they themselves had shown to be absurd. The royal prerogative as understood by Clarendon and the lawyers was sacrificed. Politically, the Tories had to accept the principles of limited monarchy, but they saved their church both from Roman catholicism and unlimited toleration. An Act of 1689 gave relief to protestant dissenters other than unitarians. They were allowed their own teachers and places of worship under certain safeguards. This was a modest price for the Tories to pay for the preservation of the Restoration policy of confining public office to churchmen. The landed and church interests retained considerable, though not exclusive, power.

The Whigs had obtained some measure of toleration for

their dissenting allies and the right for themselves to participate in politics once again. They failed in their ambition to exclude the Tories from office by the implicit assumption that Whigs were the only true guardians of the fundamental law by which the realm was governed. There was a parallel between the ideas of the extreme Whigs and the extreme Covenanters. When Halifax was accused by Hampden after 1688 for his part against the Rye House conspirators, Halifax summed up Hampden's argument in this form: if the government breaks the law, the people (that is, Hampden and his fellow conspirators) may act, for the governors are the real conspirators, and those condemned by the law in being are really murdered since they are on the side of the law, and the whole nation is guilty in permitting their murder. The people was a vague abstraction to the Whigs, and a fundamental law, as Halifax noted, was apt to be used as men use their friends, to be commended when useful, and discarded when objectionable.

Obedience in the Whig view was due to the fundamental law; they were hostile to any theory of sovereignty. Government rested upon the consent of individuals endowed with inalienable natural rights, for the preservation of which government existed. By 1688 these principles had lost their revolutionary character; the extreme doctrines associated with republicanism had disappeared as a more utilitarian attitude began to influence politics.

The effects of the Revolution on the relations of England and Scotland were gradually revealed in the years before the Act of Settlement in 1701. In Scotland, presbyterianism was permanently established and parliament increasingly expressed the growing secular interests of the country. In England, the Anglican church was supreme and parliament was concerned in the great French war. Limited monarchy had triumphed in both countries and William had to govern with two different parliaments, conscious of different interests and outlook. The course of William's reign convinced the Scots that the more limited William was by the English parliament, the less able was he to govern according to the will of his Scottish parliament. Limited monarchy in conjunction with the Union of Crowns gave to the king's English ministers the indirect rule of Scotland, and the means to sacrifice Scottish interests to English prosperity.

The poverty of Scotland compared to England was accentuated in the seventeenth century, and by 1690 the Scots were desperately aware that their future depended upon the opening of new markets for their manufactures. They had been forced to imitate the English policy of industrial protection, trade regulation and colonial development, but suffered throughout the century from "want of riches". Before 1660 only one Scotsman traded with America. Scottish trade was still European and was greatly affected by English wars with the Netherlands and France, Scotland's main commercial outlets. Before 1660, the period in which England's naval power and colonial expansion were established, Scottish economy remained bound by its still mainly medieval organization. Its economic interests were different from England's. Scottish trade was mainly in raw materials or allied rural manufactures: in 1614 the total value of exported manufactures was little more than the value of the fish exported to the continent. England's interest was already dominated by the export of cloth, and commercial rivalry with Scotland centred upon the Scottish wool exports. The English wished to obtain Scottish wool for cloth-making and to prevent the buying of English wool by the Scots for sale abroad.

The English manufacture of cloth had continued to expand and was the most important of English exports. The processes of manufacture were advanced, and the organization of the industry, based on the worker possessing the machinery but not concerned with the supply of the material or marketing of the product, became specialized and complicated. In the newer and finer kinds of cloth-making the capitalist tendency was pronounced, and it was characteristic also of new industries. Guilds and corporations ceased to regulate industry. Trade was still in the hands of the great trading companies but, with the exception of the East Indian Company, by 1700 their importance had declined and private traders were responsible for important sections of foreign trade. Colonial expansion was to exercise a decisive influence upon commercial policy. Ventures to America were financed and organized by all classes, and emigrants were stimulated by the hope of escaping from religious or economic difficulties in England. Success only followed repeated endeavours and experiments, but by 1650 settlements of varying economic, social and political character existed along the North American coast and in the West Indies.

The Commonwealth was influenced by the idea of a commercially self-sufficient empire, in which the colonies supplied English needs and were a market for English goods. It was declared that the colonies were and ought to be subordinate to and dependent on England. By the Navigation Act of 1651, goods imported from Asia, Africa and America were to be brought in English or colonial ships. Certain enumerated commodities were to be shipped directly to England, and colonists were to buy European goods only from English merchants and provided such goods had been conveyed to England by English ships or by ships of the country of origin.

This commercial policy applied to Scotland after the Cromwellian Union of 1654. Both countries were to have free trade, the same regulations of exports and imports, and the same customs, but although this policy was beneficial to England, Scottish trade was disrupted. The export of raw materials was limited and Scottish industry was unable to use the whole amount. Scottish trade was depressed by the civil wars and the cost of Cromwell's occupation. In 1660, when Scotland regained its political independence, it was excluded by the English parliament from the English commercial system because economic union, without political union, would allow Scottish merchants to evade the protective system, to share the plantation trade and, by their Dutch trade, provide an alternative channel of trade between the colonies and the Continent. In 1667 the English made it clear that Scotland's political independence prevented treatment as favourable as Ireland's. "Ireland is not only under one King with Us, as Scotland, but belongs unto and is an Appendix of the Crowne of England, ... by all which it is absolutely in our power when we grant priviledges to them to compell and keep them up to the restrictions and limitations of them, all which is quite otherwise in relacon to Scotland."

Before the Revolution, the Scottish parliament had passed

acts to encourage industry. By 1693 the country had recovered from the depression of the middle decades of the century, and industrial progress had brought its economy more into line with England's, thereby facilitating the achievement of union in 1707. The need for markets for manufactures was pressing. Parliament expressed the nation's resolve to redeem its earlier neglect of trade, and adopted the project of a Scottish colony as the means of national rehabilitation. An Act of 1693 "for Encouraging of Forraigne Trade" gave valuable privileges to any company trading abroad and promised protection against hostile action.

Some Scots and English merchants in London took advantage of the Scottish Act to propose a company which should be entitled to compete lawfully under the Scottish flag with the East Indian Company. A Scots act of 1695 authorized "a Company Tradeing to Affrica and the Indies"; but the king's Commissioner had granted greater privileges than his instructions warranted. Owing to the opposition of the English parliament and to the intervention of the king's agents abroad, the Company became a wholly Scottish concern, and decided to plant a colony on the Isthmus of Darien in the belief that it would be situated so as to obtain control of the East and West Indies trade. The complete failure of this colonial enterprise deeply stirred Scottish feeling and discredited the English connection with many, although others were convinced that there was no longer any practicable alternative to an economic agreement with England. Parliament, however, had learnt that it was able to lead the nation against the king's ministers.

The incompatibility of an independent parliament and an executive directed by English ministers was seen as the essential consequence of the Union of Crowns. In 1702 Commissioners were appointed by each country to consider ways of improving their relationship. The negotiations broke down over the grievances of the "Company Tradeing to Affrica and the Indies". The Scots had proposed a union of parliaments, but with the failure of negotiations Scottish opinion turned strongly against any form of political incorporation, and began to consider very strict limitations upon the crown in order to end the subordination of the Scottish to the English government.

The question of the succession in the event of Anne's death, decided by England in favour of the Hanoverians, was unsettled in Scotland, and became the means to threaten England. The policy of those Scottish parliamentarians opposed to the ministers was to impose certain conditions before the successor to the English throne was accepted by Scotland, and to gain their ends by withholding supplies.

This programme was successfully pursued during the first year (1703) of the last Scottish parliament because it won the support of all but those who were tied by interest to the ministers. The confusion of parties and their mutual relations was pronounced and it was only in the final debate on the Treaty of Union that the alternative of separation or of political incorporation compelled the parties to a decision. There were three main parties, shading into each other, in 1703. The ministers' party was small. Sometimes it had the support of the Revolution Whigs because their interest was bound to the preservation of the settlement of 1688: at other times the Whigs supported the Country Party because the presbyterian church was likely to be more secure if Scotland was independent of England. The Country Party wanted national independence and limitations upon the crown, and contained cavaliers or moderate Jacobites. The extreme Jacobites were anxious to increase the hostility between England and Scotland as the preliminary to a Stewart and episcopalian restoration in Scotland.

During 1703 the ministers were compelled to accept an act by which Scotland could only be committed to war with the consent of its own parliament, and they agreed, willingly enough for the sake of revenue, to an act permitting the import of wines, including French, although France and England were at war. They were unable to prevent the Country and Jacobite parties from voting the Act of Security, although with the aid of some Jacobites the proposal to include in the act such limitations upon the crown as would have virtually transformed Scotland into a republic, was rejected. The queen did not sanction the act until 1704 when the refusal of parliament to grant supplies threatened to compel the disbanding of the army at the height of the English and French war.

The government in 1704 was in the hands of the New Party,

which had broken away from the more Jacobite elements of the Country party, and had promised to settle the succession as England desired provided that all great official appointments were made with parliamentary consent. The New Party had failed completely when it had to advise the queen to sanction the Act of Security, which declared that parliament, twenty days after the death of Anne, was to choose a successor who was a protestant and a Stewart, but not the successor to the English throne, unless Scotland was granted complete freedom of government, religion and trade.

By this act and by the covert threat of a separate foreign policy, Scotland had asserted its equality with England, which was convinced by this example of parliamentary independence that the relation of England and Scotland, unless it was one of complete separation, had to continue as under the Union of Crowns or to be converted into a parliamentary union. In 1705 the English parliament passed an act, generally known as the Alien Act, which was designed to offer this choice, and to make clear the economic effects of separation.

It became evident that the Scottish parliament was not prepared to pass an Act of Succession, so that the choice became one of incorporation or separation, and the opposition was not united on separation. The New Party, out of office after 1704, was the most realistic, saw the danger of a Jacobite restoration and of damage to trade, and gave up its preference for limitation to support, without making its intentions clear, incorporation. Its action was to carry the Union, but Jacobite uncertainties also helped to paralyse the opposition.

The final treaty gave to England the security that no independent Scottish parliament should continue and threaten English foreign policy; it gave to Scotland free trade in England and the colonies, preservation of its law and courts, and certain economic and financial compensations. The Union was finally accepted in Scotland because the church, secured by an Act of Parliament which became an integral part of the Treaty of Union, ceased its active resistance and forbore to press more than its minimum claims.

It was fortunate that there had been clear-sighted and resolute men willing to take advantage of the very magnitude of the crisis in the relations of the two countries, for in the few years from 1704 to 1707 England at last learned what its true interest demanded, and Scotland, facing the desperate adventure of an independent monarchy, was held back only by the danger of Jacobitism to the last century and a half of its history. In those few years, the two countries were near enough and equal enough to arrive at a lasting understanding. In this sense, it was not 1688 but 1707 which ended the possibility of a Roman Catholic state in England and Scotland. The Reformation and the Revolution Settlement found their sequel and their guarantee in the Union of 1707. Protestantism and constitutional government were reconciled in the triumph of moderation in religion and politics over exclusive, intolerant and absolutist doctrines. The moderation and compromise of the 1688 Revolution were essential conditions of the greater compromise between the two kingdoms.

READING LIST

J. W. Allen: *A History of Political Thought in the Sixteenth Century*, London, 1928; *English Political Thought*, 1603–1660, London, 1938.

R. Baillie: *Letters and Journals* (edit. D. Laing), Edinburgh, 1841–2.

J. B. Black: *The Reign of Elizabeth*, Oxford, 1936.

P. Hume Brown: *History of Scotland*, Cambridge, 1899–1909; *The Legislative Union of England and Scotland*, Oxford, 1914.

G. N. Clark: *The Later Stuarts*, Oxford, 1937; *The Wealth of England*, London, 1946.

A. Cunningham: *The Loyal Clans*, Cambridge, 1932.

G. Davies: *The Early Stuarts*, Oxford, 1937.

A. V. Dicey & R. S. Rait: *Thoughts on the Union between England and Scotland*, London, 1920.

K. G. Feiling: *A History of the Tory Party*, 1640–1714, Oxford, 1924.

J. N. Figgis: *The Divine Right of Kings*, 2nd. edit., Cambridge, 1934.

Sir Robert Filmer: *Patriarcha* (edit. P. Laslett), Oxford, 1949.

H. C. Foxcroft: *Life and Letters of Sir George Savile*, London, 1898.

I. F. Grant: *The Social and Economic Development of Scotland to 1603*, Edinburgh, 1930; *The Economic History of Scotland*, London, 1934.

G. P. Gooch & H. J. Laski: *English Democratic Ideas in the Seventeenth Century*, Cambridge, 1927.

J. H. Hexter: *The Reign of King Pym*, Cambridge (Massachusetts), 1941.

M. A. Judson: *The Crisis of the Constitution*, New Brunswick, 1949.

Theodora Keith: *Commercial Relations of England and Scotland*, Cambridge, 1910.

John Knox's *History of the Reformation in Scotland*, edit. W. C. Dickinson, London, 1949.

A. Lang: *Sir George Mackenzie*, London, 1909.

J. G. MacGregor: *The Scottish Presbyterian Polity*, Edinburgh, 1926.

J. Mackinnon: *The Union of England and Scotland*, London, 1896; *A History of Modern Liberty*, London, 1906–41.

C. H. McIlwain: *The Political Works of James I*, Harvard University Press, 1918; *The High Court of Parliament*, New Haven, 1910.

D. Masson: *Drummond of Hawthornden*, London, 1873.

D. Mathew: *The Age of Charles I*, London, 1951.

W. L. Mathieson: *Politics and Religion*, Glasgow, 1902; *Scotland and the Union*, Glasgow, 1905.

J. E. Neale: *Queen Elizabeth*, London, 1934.

D. Ogg: *England in the Reign of Charles II*, Oxford, 1934.

R. S. Rait: *The Parliaments of Scotland*, Glasgow, 1924.

A. L. Rowse: *The England of Elizabeth*, London, 1950.

H. R. Trevor-Roper: *Archbishop Laud*, London, 1940.

Wariston, A. Johnston of: *Diary* (3 vols.), Edinburgh, 1911–40.

A. S. P. Woodhouse: *Puritanism and Liberty*, London, 1938.

INDEX

A

Act of Classes, 121, 123
Act Rescissory, 137
Act of Security, 166
Act of Settlement, 161
Alien Act, 167
Articles of Perth, 84, 89, 90
Assertory Act, 144

B

Bancroft, 71
"Bands", 33, 91
Baillie, 109, 112
Barrow, 75
Bill of Rights, 160
Black Acts, 41
Book of Canons, 90
Bothwell Bridge, 145
Brownists, 75
Buchanan, xiii, 84
Burleigh, 51, 53, 62

C

Cabal, 140
Charles I, 87, 88, 89, 91, 105, 111, 118, 120, 137
—II, 121, 127, 130, 133, 147, 151
Church and State, 37, 43, 69, 72, 103, 159
Claim of Right, 158
Clarendon, 101, 105, 132, 135, 137, 140, 147
Commons, 63, 65, 80, 86, 89, 95, 102, 134, 140, 141, 160

Congregationalists, 73–5
Convention of Estates, 32, 108, 157
—of Royal Burghs, 28, 29
Covenanters, 44, 108, 113, 121, 131, 142, 154
Craig, ix, xvi, 23, 47, 56
Cromwell, xix, 111, 118, 121, 126, 127, 132, 138

D

Danby, 147, 149, 151
Divine Right of Kings, 45, 88, 123, 129, 131, 151
— —Presbytery, xiv, 110, 122

E

Economic interests of England, 55, 57, 164
— —Scotland, 23, 27, 163, 164, 165
Elders, 36, 75, 92, 110, 112
Elizabeth, 49, 51, 52, 54, 64
Engagement, The, 118
Episcopacy, 41, 66, 83, 90, 92, 95, 98, 99, 110, 113, 136, 137, 158
Exclusion debates, 150

F

Foreign Policy, 51, 81, 138, 148, 159

INDEX

Fundamental Law, xx, 68, 79, 85, 95, 97, 117, 122, 162

G

General Assembly, 36, 37, 41, 44, 90, 91, 92, 93, 99, 107, 113, 126, 128, 130, 131
Gentry, 48, 58–60, 64, 129, 134, 152
God's Law, xii, xiii, 37, 43, 91, 101, 110, 113, 122, 142
Government and property, 79, 86, 87, 101, 144
Grand Remonstrance, 96
Grindal, 71

H

Halifax, xix, 137, 150, 151, 161, 162
Hooker, xvii, 68, 71
Hunton, xvii

I

Independents, 113, 120, 124
Indulgence, 131, 133, 144, 151, 156
Instrument of Government, 126, 127

J

James I and VI, xvi, 25, 29, 40, 41, 44–6, 77, 82, 84, 85, 86, 88
—II and VII, 129, 131, 144, 146, 152, 154, 155
Jus Populi Vindicatum, xvi, 143

K

Knox, xii, 34, 35, 38

L

Laud, 88, 89, 99, 132, 134
Lauderdale, 136, 144, 148
Law (*see* Fundamental Law and God's Law)
Levellers, xviii, 116, 117
Locke, xx, 97
Lords of the Articles, 32, 83, 91, 92, 137, 158

M

Mackenzie, Sir George, 143
Melville, xii, 40, 44, 93
Mercantilism, 55
Milton, xviii
Monk, 137
Monmouth, 145, 150, 152
Montrose, 99, 111
Morton, 40

N

National Covenant, 90, 91, 104, 110, 122, 131, 137, 142, 145
Navigation Act, 164
Nobility (Scottish), 25, 35, 38, 45, 90, 91, 119, 127, 131, 142

P

Parliament of England, 48, 49, 50, 62–4, 68–9, 80, 85, 86, 93, 94, 105, 112, 118, 120, 133, 149, 160, 161

Parliament of Scotland, 30, 82, 92, 93, 98, 119, 128, 130, 155, 158, 165
Prerogative, 29, 61, 64, 78, 84, 87, 88, 89, 92, 95, 99, 100, 106, 130, 141, 146, 150, 152
Protesters, 123
Puritanism and Puritans, 52, 65, 66, 72, 73, 75, 88, 94
Pym, 106

R

Reformation in England, 70
—Scotland, 33
Resolutioners, 123
Rutherford, xiv, 110, 112, 115

S

Second Book of Discipline, 43
Shaftesbury, 147, 148, 149
Smyth, John, 72
Solemn League and Covenant, 107, 108, 119
Sovereignty, xviii, xx, 68, 69, 80, 85, 88, 96, 100, 115, 125
Star Chamber, 61
Statute of Artificers, 55
Strafford, 95

T

Taxation, 45, 78, 85, 86, 91, 133, 138, 149, 155
Test Act, 146, 147
— —(Scottish), 154
Toleration, xiv, xxi, 23, 76, 103, 113, 114, 121, 128, 143, 146
Tories, 149, 151, 159, 161
Triennial Act—Scottish, 92 ; English, 161

U

Union of Crowns, x, 136, 157, 162, 165, 167

W

Wariston, 109, 112, 125
Westminster Assembly, xiv, 107, 112
Whigs, 130, 134, 150, 152, 159, 162
Whitelocke, 88
William III, 149, 150, 153, 157, 158, 159, 160, 161

For Product Safety Concerns and Information please contact our EU
representative GPSR@taylorandfrancis.com
Taylor & Francis Verlag GmbH, Kaufingerstraße 24, 80331 München, Germany

www.ingramcontent.com/pod-product-compliance
Lightning Source LLC
Chambersburg PA
CBHW061838300426
44115CB00013B/2440